Penguin Monarchs

THE HOUSE OF TUDOR

Henry VII	Sean Cunningham
Henry VIII	John Guy
Edward VI	Stephen Alford
Mary I	John Edwards
Elizabeth I	Helen Castor

THE HOUSE OF STUART

James I	Thomas Cogswell
Charles I	Mark Kishlansky
[Cromwell	David Horspool]
Charles II	Clare Jackson
James II	David Womersley
William III & Mary II	Jonathan Keates
Anne	Richard Hewlings

THE HOUSE OF HANOVER

George I	Tim Blanning
George II	Norman Davies
George III	Amanda Foreman
George IV	Stella Tillyard
William IV	Roger Knight
Victoria	Jane Ridley

THE HOUSES OF SAXE-COBURG & GOTHA AND WINDSOR

Edward VII	Richard Davenport-Hines
George V	David Cannadine
Edward VIII	Piers Brendon
George VI	Philip Ziegler
Elizabeth II	Douglas Hurd

TIM BLANNING

George I

The Lucky King

ALLEN LANE

an imprint of

PENGUIN BOOKS

ALLEN LANE

UK | USA | Canada | Ireland | Australia
India | New Zealand | South Africa

Penguin Books is part of the Penguin Random House group of companies
whose addresses can be found at global.penguinrandomhouse.com

First published 2017
001

Copyright © Tim Blanning, 2017

The moral right of the author has been asserted

Set in 9.5/13.5 pt Sabon LT Std
Typeset by Jouve (UK), Milton Keynes
Printed in Great Britain by Clays Ltd, St Ives plc

ISBN: 978-0-141-97683-9

www.greenpenguin.co.uk

Contents

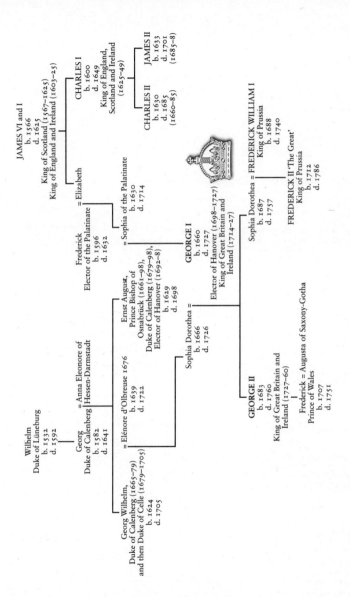

George I

I
Hanover

George I (or 'Georg Ludwig', as he should be known until his accession in 1714) was not the most exciting of the eleven Hanoverians to have reigned in the United Kingdom, but he was probably the most important. He was certainly the luckiest.

When he was born, on 28 May 1660, his prospects were very modest. His father, Ernst August, was the youngest of the four sons of the Duke of Brunswick-Lüneburg, and the best he could hope for was to become the Prince-Bishop of Osnabrück. As this benefice was non-hereditary, Ernst August would have nothing to pass on to his son apart from pride in an ancient lineage. Tracing back to the eighth century, the Guelphs of Brunswick had enjoyed one period of glory in the mid twelfth century – under Duke Henry 'the Lion' (1129–95) – but that had ended in disaster. Confined subsequently to north-west Germany and the region between the Weser and Elbe rivers, they compounded their misfortunes by repeatedly dividing their territories among their male offspring. It was Georg Ludwig's first stroke of luck that his father, uncles and cousins agreed to impose primogeniture on future generations, a sensible move from which he himself proved to be the ultimate beneficiary, thanks to a series of early deaths among his relations. Resisted tenaciously by the disinherited dukes, it was not until 1705 that all the Brunswick-Lüneburg lands were finally united. Although 'Brunswick-Lüneburg' remained the correct appellation, the composite principality would from now on be almost always known as 'Hanover', after its capital city.

A second inheritance of immense value bequeathed by his father, whom he succeeded in 1698, was the status and title of 'Elector of the Holy Roman Empire'. This should have been a straightforward bargain: in return for Emperor Leopold I granting the promotion in 1692, Ernst August had supplied him with 9,000 troops, 500,000 talers in cash and agreement to join the Grand Alliance against Louis XIV.[1] Alas, many years were to pass and much more money had to be spent before the grant of the title was recognized by the other electors, who were understandably reluctant to add to their number. There were eight of them, three ecclesiastical – the Archbishops of Mainz, Trier and Cologne – and five secular – Bohemia, Saxony, the Palatinate, Bavaria and Brandenburg. As the name suggests, it was their right to elect the Holy Roman Emperor, a right that was still very much alive, even though in practice a Habsburg had always been chosen for the past two and a half centuries. It was not until 1708 that Georg Ludwig finally gained admission to the electoral college, by which time the total bill had grown to about 2,000,000 talers.

It says a good deal for the prosperity of the Guelph lands, and the efficiency of their administration, that Ernst August was able to raise the funds needed for this exercise.

Moreover, it was accompanied by lavish expenditure on his court. Admittedly, he was starting from a low base. Hanover had only been the capital since 1636 and the ducal residence was a converted monastery – 'a terrible, filthy dump' was the verdict of Ernst August's duchess, Sophia, even after its conversion to a 'palace'.[2] Hemmed in by the River Leine and private dwellings, the site resisted improvement. Ernst August did his best, creating a new assembly room (*Rittersaal*) and one of the grandest opera houses north of the Alps, big enough to seat 1,300 and equipped with all the latest stage machinery. It was opened in 1689 in a blaze of representational display, the first work to be performed being Agostino Steffani's specially commissioned *Henrico Leone* (Henry the Lion), an operatic reminder of past greatness and present ambition.[3] Opera was a taste acquired by Ernst August on one of his many visits to Venice, his favoured playground. According to his wife he was 'besotted' with the city and fell into a deep depression if unable to visit for any reason.[4] The Foscari Palace on the Grand Canal was rented on a long lease, a fleet of gondolas was hired and subscriptions taken out for all the main opera houses. The enormous sums required by these annual trips were raised by the simple expedient of hiring out Hanoverian soldiers to the Republic of Venice for its wars against the Turks.[5] Their involuntary sacrifices – most never saw Hanover again – allowed Ernst August to balance his books, enjoy himself and pass on to his son sound finances.[6]

So cramped was the space in the centre of Hanover that the palace there could have no garden. Amends were made by the creation outside the town of one of the great formal gardens of Europe: Herrenhausen. Chiefly responsible was Ernst August's long-lived wife Sophia (1630–1714). By the time she had finished, the main garden was 450 metres wide and 800 metres long, bounded on three sides by canals and covering an area as large as the whole town of Hanover.[7] An eclectic mixture of Dutch, French and Venetian influences, it included spectacular water features, a great number of statues and a garden theatre still in use today.[8] A justly celebrated bird's-eye view of the gardens dating from 1708 also shows a (surprisingly modest) palace, stables and orangeries. Herrenhausen performed two main functions. It provided a welcome relief from the foetid air of downtown Hanover, especially during the summer months, and it proclaimed to visitors the splendour of the newly promoted Electors of Hanover. As Sophia proclaimed: 'only with the Herrenhausen gardens can we flaunt ourselves'.[9]

When he died in 1698, Ernst August bequeathed Herrenhausen to his widow as her personal property. With a characteristic blend of generosity and shrewdness, she passed it straight on to her son Georg Ludwig – but only on the condition that he paid for its upkeep. By all accounts – and there are many – she was a truly remarkable woman. Highly intelligent, resourceful, good-natured, down to earth and blessed with a sharp sense of humour, she charmed everyone she met. As her mother was the 'Winter Queen', Elizabeth of Bohemia (née Stuart, the daughter of James I of England), she had been brought up in the school of hard knocks, enduring poverty and insecurity during the family's long exile in the Dutch Republic. Originally, she had been earmarked as a bride for Ernst August's elder brother Georg Wilhelm, but after an 'indisposition' (presumably a venereal infection) had rendered the latter temporarily unable to procreate, she had to be switched, a decision she accepted with the cheery observation 'if one doesn't have what one loves, one has to love what one has'.[10] In the same vein was the advice she gave to her daughter Sophia Charlotte, when about to be married to the Crown Prince of Brandenburg, not to allow a marital quarrel to become a crisis, or, as she put it: 'don't make a thunderclap out of a fart'.[11]

Both Ernst August and Sophia enjoyed a generally good relationship with their eldest son and heir, Georg Ludwig. The former called him 'my Benjamin' and thought well enough of him to take him campaigning at the age of fifteen, while Sophia assured her correspondents that behind a reserved exterior her son was a sensitive, sincere and often jolly young man.[12] Perhaps their most important legacy was a tolerant attitude towards religion. Sophia was the daughter of a Calvinist father and an Anglican mother, was married to a Lutheran, had been educated in the latitudinarian atmosphere of the Dutch court and was a lifelong friend of the ecumenical philosopher Leibniz, so had a famously relaxed attitude to doctrinal differences. She told the British envoy, Lord Strafford, that, for her, all branches of Christianity were equal so long as they were directed against the '*antichrétien universal*', by which she meant the pope.[13] Her cousin, King James II of England, complained to her brother (the Elector of the Palatinate) that she had no religion at all, although it should be borne in mind that, as a zealous Catholic convert, James did set the piety bar very high.[14]

Against this supportive and enlightened upbringing has to be set a disastrous choice of bride for Georg Ludwig in 1682. It stemmed from the dynasty's determination to consolidate all the Brunswick-Lüneburg territories under one reigning prince. To this end, Ernst August's older brother, Georg Wilhelm, had agreed not to marry. This well-laid plan was then derailed when he fell in love with a French Huguenot lady, Eléonore d'Olbreuse, who became his mistress in 1664 and gave birth to a daughter, Sophia Dorothea, two years later. Once the latter had been legitimized in 1674 and her parents had married in 1676, she became heiress to Georg Ludwig's duchy of Celle. The only solution to this conundrum was for the two first cousins to get married and unite their inheritances. As Georg Ludwig had given an early indication of heterosexual enthusiasm by impregnating the governess of his sister when only sixteen, and as Sophia Dorothea grew up to be an attractive, shapely blonde with an engaging personality, the way seemed clear. However, there was much heart-searching over what was clearly a *mésalliance* between a scion of the oldest dynasty in the Holy Roman Empire and the offspring of minor French gentry.[15]

Awareness that the duchy of Celle was larger and more populous than Hanover helped Georg Ludwig to overcome the 'repugnance' he felt at marrying so far down the social scale. As his mother explained: 'he would marry a cripple if he thought it was to his advantage, because his conduct will always be governed by the interest of his dynasty'.[16] It was not, however, a solid foundation on which to build a marriage. Although two children were produced, it was not long before indifference and then hostility became apparent. Sophia Dorothea was a vivacious, light-hearted, irresponsible teenager, only sixteen when she married. Although only twenty-two, Georg Ludwig was old beyond his years, taciturn, serious, anything but fun-loving. Often away at the wars, when he returned he spent most of his waking hours hunting. His strong sexual drive was satisfied by ladies of the court, especially by Baroness Melusine von der Schulenburg, the daughter of a Brandenburg nobleman of ancient lineage. Their relationship began no later than 1691, for she gave birth to their daughter in January 1692.[17]

It was deemed quite normal for a male prince to take a mistress – indeed, even some of those who were not that way inclined felt obliged to follow the fashion – but absolutely not acceptable for a married princess to stray. In 1689 Sophia Dorothea made the acquaintance of Count Philipp Christoph von Königsmarck, a handsome young officer who had just entered Hanoverian service. His was a family with a scandalous past and a notorious future. In 1682 his elder brother had narrowly escaped the gallows in London for complicity in the murder of Thomas ('Tom of Ten Thousand') Thynne, his rival in love; his beautiful sister Aurora was to become the mistress of Augustus the Strong of Saxony-Poland and the mother of the Maréchal de Saxe, the most successful French general of the eighteenth century. For his part, Philipp Christoph certainly shared the family's taste for dangerous liaisons. He wrote his first love letter to Sophia Dorothea in 1690 while campaigning in Flanders and consummated their relationship in 1692.[18]

In a court and town the size of Hanover, their affair could not be kept secret, especially not in view of the intensity of their passion, expressed in hundreds of letters. What exactly happened in Hanover on the night of 11–12 July 1694 will never be known. According to the most probable scenario, Königsmarck went to the palace late at night for a tryst with the princess, was intercepted and hacked to death. His body was then weighted with stones and thrown into the River Leine, never to be seen again. The assassins were two high-ranking courtiers, Wilken von Klencke and Philip Adam von Eltz, and two less reputable characters, Johann Christoph von Stubenvol and Nicolò di Montalban. The main perpetrator was probably the last-named, an Italian priest and notorious rake who lived by his wits at the court as librettist, building project manager and general factotum.

How much did the elector and his family know? Nothing is certain because they knew how to keep a secret – if there was one. The official line was that Königsmarck had simply disappeared, left Hanover, gone somewhere else, who knew where, none of our business, nothing to do with us. There was no body, so no evidence of any crime. But of course tongues wagged, and would have wagged even harder if they had known about the payments made to Montalban. Although deeply in debt and eking out a living on an annual salary of 200 talers, in the same year the princely sum of 15,000 talers was credited to his account with the court Treasury.[19] So the elector, Ernst August, whose authorization for this payment would have been needed, was at least an accessory after the fact. There is no evidence that his son was an accomplice at any level: he was in Berlin at the time of the murder, although that proves nothing.[20] What is certain is that he chose never to see his wife again.

Although the correspondence uncovered by a search of Sophia Dorothea's apartments provided unequivocal evidence, she was divorced not for adultery but for her refusal to cohabit with her husband. She was then returned to her father, Duke Georg Wilhelm of Celle, who in effect placed her under house arrest in a manor house at Ahlden, a small village in the depths of the Lower Saxon countryside. There she remained for the next thirty-two years until her death in 1726, living in a confinement that was comfortable but isolated and closely guarded. Despite frequent pleas, she was never permitted to see her two children, aged ten and seven at the time of her disgrace.

So mismatched was the unhappy couple that constant cohabitation might only have made a bad situation worse. In the event, the neglected wife had both motive and opportunity to look elsewhere for affection, because her husband was away at the wars so often and for so long. This dimension needs to be stressed, for, of all the kings of England, the most militarized was George I, a professional soldier for most of his adult life. This was his *métier*, as it was for any German prince not disqualified by physical or psychological limitations. George had neither:

although a bit on the short side, he was strong, tough, courageous and a good horseman. There were plenty of wars for him to fight. In 1661, one year after George's birth, Louis XIV had taken personal control of French policy and set off in search of military *gloire*. For most of the rest of his long reign he was at war or preparing for war, the main target being the Habsburg territories in the Holy Roman Empire. At the other end of Europe, a reinvigorated Ottoman Empire had embarked on a fresh wave of expansion in the Balkans, which in 1683 took them to the very gates of Vienna.

All that made work for the fighting man to do, and Georg Ludwig started young. He saw action for the first time on 11 August 1675, at the age of fifteen, when he fought alongside his father at the Battle of the Bridge of Konz, at the junction of the Saar and Moselle rivers. An episode in the long-running conflict between Louis XIV and the Dutch Republic, this was a sharp engagement involving around 30,000 troops and ending in the complete rout of the French army. Across the Holy Roman Empire, contemporaries celebrated this first humbling of the 'Sun King'. Although highly improbable, it was reported that Louis had torn his hair and cried, 'Varus, Varus, give me back my legions!', imitating the Roman Emperor Augustus's reaction to the news of Herman the German's victory in the Teutoburg Forest in AD 9. It was also hailed as a triumph for the house of Brunswick-Lüneburg, for the army was commanded by Georg Wilhelm and his brother Ernst August.[21]

Georg Ludwig went campaigning in each of the next

three years too, until the war ended with the treaties of Nijmegen of 1678–9. Less than a year after his marriage in November 1682 he was off to the wars again, this time to fight in a battle of world-historical significance. On 11–12 September 1683 a multinational force commanded by King John Sobieski of Poland-Lithuania comprehensively defeated the Turkish army that had been besieging the Habsburg capital for the past two months. The courier who rushed back across the Holy Roman Empire to Hanover was just able to gasp out the glad tidings before dropping down dead (probably not in *conscious* imitation of Pheidippides, who expired after running the 26 miles and 385 yards from Marathon to Athens in 490 BC).[22]

Vienna had been besieged once before, in 1529, but this time the Turks were sent packing for good. In the years that followed, the Habsburgs and their German allies pursued a *reconquista* of Hungary, most of which had been under Ottoman rule since 1541. Georg Ludwig and his Hanoverian contingents played an active and often distinguished part, notably in 1685 at the Battle of Gran (Esztergom) on the Danube and in the ensuing capture of Neuhäusel (Nové Zámky).[23] Less glorious was participation in the Nine Years War (1688–97), when Georg Ludwig went campaigning against the French again in the Low Countries in the army commanded by William III. He found himself on the losing side at Fleurus in 1690, Steenkerken in 1692 and Neerwinden in 1693.[24] It was perhaps with a sense of relief that he returned to Hanover in 1695 to take over the government of the electorate from his increasingly incapacitated father. In 1700, by this time elector, he emerged from retirement to command the army sent to dislodge the Danes from the duchy of Holstein-Gottorp.[25]

He was to enjoy one last blaze of military glory in 1707 at a critical time during the War of the Spanish Succession. With Prince Eugene busy in Italy and Marlborough in the Low Countries, the allies were desperate to find a competent general to take command on the Upper Rhine. Georg Ludwig drove a hard bargain, agreeing to serve only on condition that the Catholic electors dropped their obstruction of Hanover's admission to the electoral college. In truth, he did not need to do much in return. Arriving at the front in September, he issued a new disciplinary code, reorganized the defensive lines and beat off a French raiding force. The French general, the duc de Villars, then obligingly went back across the Rhine and into winter quarters.[26] For this modest feat of arms, Georg Ludwig was hailed by the pamphleteers as 'Saviour of the Empire'.

In 1708 Eugene and Marlborough concentrated their efforts on the Low Countries, where they won a great victory over the French at Oudenarde on 11 July. Among the many who distinguished themselves that day with feats of valour was Georg Ludwig's eldest son, Georg August, whom he had sent to Marlborough's camp to learn the art of war. He led the Hanoverian cavalry forming part of General Cadogan's vanguard, was engaged in hand-to-hand fighting, and was reported to have had a horse shot under him and a fellow officer killed alongside him.[27] This was a story that grew with the telling, especially when propagandists of the Hanoverian succession in England were doing the telling. The presence of the Stuart Pretender at the battle on the *French* side was naturally exploited to the full, not least because his inactivity as a distant observer of the conflict was in such sharp contrast to Georg August's heroic role. Jonathan Swift's ode to the victory included the lines:

> Not so did behave
> Young Hanover brave
> In this bloody Field,
> I assure ye
> When his War-horse was shot
> He valued it not
> But fought still on foot
> Like a Fury.[28]

Back on the Rhine, Georg Ludwig was left short of men, short of supplies and short of esteem. He put up with this enforced inactivity for another year and then resigned his command in a huff in December 1709.[29]

That marked the end of his military career, but by then it had served its purpose. Along the way, he had acquired first-hand knowledge, not only of warfare but of the most important contested areas in Europe – the Baltic, the Low Countries, the Rhineland and the Balkans. This was to serve him well when he took charge of British foreign policy in 1714 and was faced with a Jacobite rebellion in 1715. He had raised the prestige of the Hanoverian armed forces in Europe and had established good relations with Austrian, Dutch and English decision-makers. With his admission to the highest college of the Holy Roman Empire, Georg Ludwig was now every inch an elector. It would also burnish his credentials as a future British king. In the course of the wars of the late seventeenth century, the Hanoverian dukes had acquired the well-deserved reputation of being Christian warriors. Of Georg Ludwig's five brothers, three died in battle fighting the Turks or the French and a fourth became an imperial field marshal. For a British audience it was especially important that a numerous Hanoverian contingent had fought on the right side with distinction and died in large numbers at the Battle of Blenheim in August 1704.[30] So the Hanoverian pamphleteers hailed him as 'well versed in the Art of War, and of invincible Courage, having often expos'd his Person to the greatest Dangers, in *Hungary*, in the *Morea*, on the *Rhine*, and in *Flanders*'.[31]

2

The Hanoverian Succession in England

All who met George's mother, the Dowager Electress Sophia, agreed that she was the ornament of her age. In the opinion of the Duchess of Württemberg: 'she is probably the most agreeable and cleverest person in the world and it is a great pleasure for anyone who has the honour to consort with her, for she is very good-natured and clever to a degree, so much so that everyone should take her as a model'.[1] Her astuteness extended to the timing of her departure from the world she had graced for so long. On 28 May 1714, while taking a stroll at Herrenhausen, a sudden shower sent her running for cover, whereupon she collapsed and died eleven days later at the age of eighty-three. For the past twelve years she had been heir apparent to the English, Scottish and Irish thrones, as the closest Protestant relation of Queen Anne. Following the death of the latter's only surviving child, the Duke of Gloucester, the Act of Settlement of 1701 had stated that if, as seemed certain, the queen were blessed with no further issue, then 'the most excellent princess Sophia, and the heirs of her body, being Protestants' should succeed.[2] Although denying any regal ambitions, Sophia kept a sharp eye on her prospects, greeting the Act of Settlement with a medal depicting her own image on one side and on the other that of her remote ancestor Matilda, daughter of Henry II of England and wife of the great Guelph Duke Henry the Lion. Her hope for an invitation to England was frustrated by Queen Anne's understandable reluctance to install a rival centre of power, strengthened by the further objection that the presence of her successor would force her 'to look at her coffin every day that remained of her life'. [3]

Queen Anne outlived Sophia by barely two months, dying on 1 August 1714. Had the order of fatalities been reversed, who knows what might have happened in London. Whether the aged Sophia would have been willing or able to make the arduous journey across Germany and the Netherlands to her new realm must be doubted. In the event, it was her hale and hearty son who took charge, although he was in no hurry to arrive. It was not until 18 September that the royal yacht docked at Greenwich. George had wanted to come ashore without fuss at what was then the remote port of Harwich, but had been persuaded not to miss a public relations opportunity. A member of his entourage recorded that their passage up the Thames in the gloaming was brightened in both senses by illuminations on both banks. Two days later George set out for London, accompanied by a procession so extended that it took half the day to pass.[4] Watching in the City from a stand erected by the Grocers' Company was the antiquarian Ralph Thoresby, who wrote in his diary: 'we had a fair view of the cavalcade when his Majesty, King George, made his public entry through the city, which was most splendid and magnificent above expression, the nobility even burdened with gold and silver embroidery. We counted above two hundred and six coaches, though there were frequently two lords in one coach, besides the Bishops and Judges, &c.; at last came the most blessed sight of a Protestant King and Prince (whom I had a full view of) attended with the loud acclamations of the people.'[5]

Beneath this smooth surface of public celebration, tumultuous conflict seethed. During the previous few weeks, London had been the scene of frantic agitation for and against the Hanoverian succession. Ever since the Glorious Revolution of 1688 had sent James II fleeing into French exile, to be replaced by his daughter Mary and her husband William of Orange, the 'Jacobite' supporters of the deposed king had conspired to bring about his return, by fair means or foul. The death of Queen Anne, Mary's sister, was widely expected to be the signal for a violent attempt to secure a Stuart restoration. Although James II had died in 1701, his claim had passed to his eldest son, also called James and styled 'James III' by the Jacobites and 'The Pretender' by everyone else. His prospects in the summer of 1714 looked promising, for he enjoyed support at the very heart of government. For some years, rumours had been circulating that Queen Anne was secretly promoting her half-brother's cause. They were not accurate, but they were widely believed.[6] Her adamant refusal to allow Georg Ludwig's eldest son, Georg August (the future George II), to move to England to safeguard the Hanoverian interest was thought to be especially ominous. As her health weakened in 1713, Jacobite agitation intensified. Since the autumn of that year, both the leading figures in the Tory administration, in office since 1710, the Earl of Oxford (Robert Harley) and Viscount Bolingbroke (Henry St John), had been corresponding secretly and separately with the Jacobite court-in-exile at Saint Germain in France.[7]

The eventual failure of the Jacobites should not be allowed to diminish the appeal of their creed. They had a good case when they argued that James II remained the lawful sovereign after 1688 for the good reason that they believed his title came from God. As the eldest living legitimate son of Charles I, he had an 'indefeasible right' to the crown which no human agency could remove. And the same applied to his own son, James III. Those who opposed them were traitors to both their king and their God. Plentiful indeed were the biblical references to support such a view, the most popular being St Paul's Epistle to the Romans, chapter thirteen, verse two: 'Whosoever therefore resisteth the power, resisteth the ordinance of God: and they that resist shall receive to themselves damnation.' So the Jacobite package – the divine right of kings, the indefeasible right of hereditary succession and non-resistance – was underpinned by a logic with a powerful appeal to those who accepted the premises.

Against it, the supporters of the Hanoverian succession could muster cogent arguments of their own. Firstly, there was the question of heredity. Jacobites at the time, and neo-Jacobite historians since, have made much play with the statistic that it was not just the Pretender who had a superior hereditary claim to the Hanoverians: there were *fifty-three* others better qualified. This would not be the first time that a statistic has been abused. Georg Ludwig was not 'a distant descendant' of the Stuarts or 'absurdly remote from the hereditary line', as two recent historians (who ought to have known better) put it. The Electress Sophia was in fact the *granddaughter* of James I and the *niece* of Charles I. The much-vaunted claims of the fifty-three claimants were superior solely on account of their date of birth. In terms of *consanguinity*, these other French, Italian or Savoyard families were no more Stuart than were the Hanoverians.[8]

Better qualified by birth they may have been, but they were disqualified by religion, for they were all Catholics and the Act of Settlement stated that no Catholic could succeed. Moreover, that Act had been passed almost unanimously by a House of Commons in which the Tories enjoyed a majority and with only five peers dissenting in the upper house.[9] As this indicated, the Glorious Revolution had initiated a paradigm shift: Parliament was now quite clear that it could settle succession by statute.[10] All kinds of verbal fudges were deployed to soften the blow to sensitive consciences, but the fact remained that hereditary divine right had died when James II fled his kingdom. In its place came reason of state, whose most potent ingredient was hostility to Roman Catholicism, tersely summarized by the Convention Parliament of 1689: 'it hath been found, by experience, to be inconsistent with the safety and welfare of this Protestant Kingdom, to be governed by a Popish Prince'. The three disastrous years of James II's reign confirmed the long-held suspicion harboured by most of his subjects that Catholicism threatened not just Protestantism but also liberty and property. Although they comprised only around 1 per cent of the population of England, Catholics loomed very large in the English demonology. In Hugh Trevor-Roper's caustic verdict: 'there were a hundred thousand men ready to rise in arms against Popery, without knowing whether Popery were a man or a horse'.[11]

Closely allied was Francophobia. As one French observer lamented about the English: 'before they learn there is a God to be served, they learn that there are Frenchmen to be detested, and the first words they utter are curses against us, the Pretender and the Pope'.[12] What was to prove a durable prejudice harked back to Louis XIV, whose aggressive militarism went hand in hand with domination of his servile Stuart relations and persecution of his Protestant subjects. It was a symbiosis expressed well by the House of Lords in a collective declaration in 1702: 'All true Englishmen, since the decay of the Spanish monarchy, have taken it for granted that the security of their religion, liberty and property, that their honour, their wealth and their trade, depend chiefly on the measures to be taken from time to time against the growing power of France.'[13]

The last ingredient in this stew of anti-Jacobite prejudice was the firmly held belief that Catholicism equalled poverty while Protestantism equalled prosperity. A trope of the prolific pamphlet literature was the allegation that the French lived on '*soupe maigre*' (hot water with a bit of fat added), 'grass' (the contemptuous name for salad) and frogs, and wore wooden shoes. Dietary and vestiary nationalism is not always given the attention it deserves, but it was certainly common in early-eighteenth-century England. Typical of the genre was an anti-Jacobite pamphlet of 1716, threatening that the Pretender's regime would mean a diet of brown bread and water and a wardrobe consisting simply of 'caddos' – the rough woollen jerkins favoured by 'the wild Irish' – and wooden shoes.[14] The other side of the coin, of course, was the belief that the commercial prosperity enjoyed by the beef-eating English and their Dutch allies derived from, and was dependent on, their Protestantism.

In short, the new king's greatest asset was his religion and the fact that he was not James II's son. He was a Stuart on his mother's side, but he was a *Protestant* Stuart. That he was a Lutheran Protestant troubled few. Although some Jacobites tried to argue, rather disingenuously, that consubstantiation was almost the same as transubstantiation and expressed the hope that 'The *Lutheran* Churches approach somewhat too much the *Romish* Superstition, in some points of Doctrine and Ceremony, to meet with a favourable Reception here',[15] everyone knew that Martin Luther had been the rock of the Reformation and the scourge of popery. To allay any remaining doubts, King George was careful to attend Anglican services and to take Communion in the Anglican rite as soon as he arrived. When he returned to Hanover, as he did six times during the course of his reign, he was equally careful to take with him an Anglican chaplain and to ensure that his attendance at Anglican services while abroad was reported in the English press.[16]

During those crucial few weeks at the beginning of his reign, George also benefited from the enterprise shown by his English supporters in securing his throne. Their task proved to be not as formidable as they had feared or the Jacobites had hoped. Oxford and Bolingbroke's flirtation with the Jacobite exiles at Saint Germain had been motivated more by a wish to ensure the support of Jacobite Tories in Parliament than by any real desire to bring in the Pretender.[17] Bolingbroke bluntly told 'James III' that he had no chance of succeeding unless he abandoned his Catholic faith, adding that the English would rather have the 'Grand Turk' for their sovereign than a papist.[18] His cause was not helped by the vicious feud between Oxford and Bolingbroke, eventually won by the latter but not until Queen Anne was at death's door. As Bolingbroke lamented: 'The Earl of Oxford was removed on Tuesday; the Queen died on Sunday. What a world is this and how does Fortune banter us,' adding in a letter to Jonathan Swift, 'The fruit turned rotten at the very moment it grew ripe.'[19] His opponents would have been too quick for him, even if he had tried to frustrate the Hanoverians. Shortly before she finally lost consciousness, the old queen was induced to make the Duke of Shrewsbury Lord Treasurer. Even before she had drawn her last choking breath, Shrewsbury and the Dukes of Argyll and Somerset had wrested control from Bolingbroke. The Privy Council they summoned immediately took decisive action, sending troops to occupy key positions in the capital, closing ports and sending off a courier to Hanover to announce the impending succession.[20]

Already discredited across the political spectrum by his flagrant debauchery and free-thinking, Bolingbroke had no prospect of mounting an insurrection.[21] When Francis Atterbury, the Jacobite Bishop of Rochester, offered to proclaim the Pretender at Charing Cross, Bolingbroke told him it was pointless. 'Never was a better cause lost for want of spirit!' was Atterbury's disgusted response.[22] But Bolingbroke was right. Popular agitation for a Stuart restoration was conspicuous by its absence in the summer of 1714. Two weeks after Queen Anne's death, he recorded ruefully: 'there never was yet so quiet a transition from one government to another . . . for we are at this moment in as perfect tranquillity as ever'.[23] Nor was any action to be expected from the political elite. The Whigs in Parliament were united in their opposition to a Stuart restoration, but the Tory Party was hopelessly divided. As many as seventy-five of the latter's MPs could be classified as 'Hanoverian Tories', that is to say they would refuse to accept the Pretender even if he abandoned Catholicism.[24] As Geoffrey Holmes sagely commented: 'a majority of Tories were Jacobite by conviction but Hanoverian by caution' ('Hanoverian when sober, Jacobite when drunk' was Edward Gregg's alternative version).[25]

In short, George's accession proceeded as smoothly as oil and butter. Given the wild volatility of English politics during the previous quarter-century, this harmony could not be expected to last. An early indication of what was to come was the widespread rioting that erupted on coronation day, 20 October 1714. These were not Jacobite demonstrations, rather High Church attacks on Nonconformist meeting houses and the first populist shots in the election campaign for the new Parliament that by law had to be summoned within six months of Queen Anne's death.[26] In Hanover, the Estates played an important role in the financial affairs of the electorate, but all the emphasis was on firm direction from above and compliant co-operation from below.[27] Nothing had prepared George for the rough and tumble of the 'rage of parties' that made Westminster politics so invigoratingly divisive and confrontational.

Safe navigation around the rocks and sandbanks of this alien new world was impeded by George's ignorance of the English language.[28] As he had known for more than a decade that he would succeed to the throne, his failure to prepare himself linguistically was both foolish and irresponsible. It may also have played a part in his clumsy handling of English party politics during the first part of his reign. For years, Whigs had sought to persuade him that only they were to be trusted, because all Tories were either outright Jacobites or fellow travellers. George was all the more ready to believe this semi-demi-truth because he had been outraged by the Peace of Utrecht, concluded by the Tory ministry in 1713 to put an end to British participation in the War of the Spanish Succession. This he regarded, not unreasonably, as a traitorous desertion of the Emperor Charles VI, the Holy Roman Empire and, not least, himself. Together with the emperor, George went on fighting the French for another year and blamed what turned out to be a disastrous final campaign on the unilateral withdrawal of the British contingents.[29]

On his arrival in London, George sent out a mixed message on his attitude to parties. Although Oxford and

Bolingbroke, the main architects of the Peace of Utrecht, were promptly dismissed, a number of Hanoverian Tories were co-opted to the Council of Regency and one of them – the Earl of Nottingham – was made Lord President of the council. This olive branch was not accepted. When two leading Tories, William Bromley and Sir Thomas Hanmer, declined the royal offer of lucrative offices, they also seemed to indicate that there was no point in wooing a party that had gone into opposition. Now the gloves came off and a systematic purge of Tories from both central and county offices began.[30] The flight of Bolingbroke to France in March 1715 and his subsequent appointment as the Pretender's Secretary of State completed the association in George's mind of Toryism with Jacobitism. Inherited by his son and successor, this assumption was to shape English politics until George's great-grandson succeeded as George III in 1760.

In the short term, it proved to be a serious mistake. It was the belief that all legal doors to advancement had been slammed shut that sent many fundamentally loyal Tories across the way to subversion. Representative was the fate of the Tory Lieutenant-General John Richmond Webb MP, who had served with distinction in the War of the Spanish Succession. Shortly after his arrival in England, George was urged to dismiss him, but in reply 'askd if he had not done his Duty well in his several posts, wch cou'd not be denied. Then the King said he wou'd have no regard to people's private piques, and ordered Web to be continued.'[31] By the following year, George had changed his mind. Webb was dismissed from his position as Governor of the Isle of

Wight and also from his regiment. With nothing to lose, he turned his loyalty across the water to the Pretender.

Webb confined his Jacobitism to truculent opposition in the House of Commons, an example of prudence that was followed by most of the purged Tory officers. Of the few prepared to risk their necks for the cause, the most eminent was the Duke of Ormonde, Captain-General and Commander-in-Chief of the British army. Dismissed by George and impeached by Parliament for his undoubted Jacobite sympathies, he fled to France in the summer of 1715, intending to return to lead the insurrection planned for the autumn. In England this proved to be a fiasco. On 20 July 1715, on receipt of a report from the British ambassador at Versailles, the Earl of Stair, that an invasion was imminent, the government took swift action. Habeas corpus was suspended, leading Jacobites were taken into custody, key garrisons strengthened, the county militias called out, twenty-one new regiments raised and 6,000 Dutch troops summoned.[32] All this proved enough to stifle the insurrection planned for the West Country. When Ormonde himself arrived in Plymouth, instead of the enthusiastic welcome he had been led to expect he found no one willing even to give him a bed for the night (or so Bolingbroke later claimed).[33] He returned to France with his tail between his legs.

Further north, Jacobite rebellions did break out. On 6 September the Pretender's standard was raised in Aberdeenshire and a month later in Northumberland. Sensibly, the government decided to deal with the English insurrection first. The task was made easier by the incompetence

displayed by the totally inexperienced Jacobite com-
mander, William Forster. Linking up with a Scottish
contingent, he led his volunteers west to Lancashire,
counting on enlisting reinforcements from the county's
numerous Catholic recusant gentry and their tenants. In
that he enjoyed some success, but when confronted by a
modest government force at Preston he offered only
half-hearted resistance before surrendering uncondition-
ally on 14 November.[34]

The Jacobites in Scotland turned out to be made of
sterner stuff, driven by an ancient sense of grievance
recently sharpened by the Act of Union of 1707. In the
course of 1715–16, perhaps as many as 20,000 Scottish
Jacobites were under arms. Yet they fatally failed to con-
centrate, being rather 'an amoeba-like drifting together of
elements'.[35] Only half that number could be mustered at
Sheriffmuir on 13 November 1715 when the Earl of Mar
sought to move south into the Lowlands. They should have
been enough, for his opponent and fellow Scottish gran-
dee, the Duke of Argyll, had only just over 3,000 under his
command. Although both sides could claim they had won
the day, strategically the verdict was decisive, for, when
Mar retreated back to Perth, any chance of an eventual
Jacobite victory went with him.[36] Over the next few
months, the army fell apart and dispersed. Their morale
was not improved by the belated arrival of the Pretender
from France on 22 December. The disillusionment was
mutual: Mar had promised to receive him with a large and
victorious army; the Pretender had promised to bring with
him arms, ammunition, money and a numerous staff of

veterans. Neither delivered.[37] The Pretender was not the man to restore a cause that was losing by the day, making but a feeble impression on his followers: 'a tall lean blak man, loukes half dead alredy, very thine, long faced, and very ill cullored and melancholy' was the verdict of the Countess of Lauderdale.[38] By then – 14 January 1716 – he had plenty to be melancholy about. He had reached Scone, just outside Perth, but his 'army' had dwindled to just 4,000 and it was known that a government force was advancing from the south. On 3 February he fled to France, never to return.

The 'Fifteen' was over. There were four main reasons for its failure. The most important was the unity of purpose shown by the English establishment. On the day that Stair's dispatch reached London, announcing an imminent rebellion, George went straight to Parliament to call for urgent action. He was rewarded with loyal addresses voted through without a dissenting voice, and then backed up at once by the firm defensive actions listed earlier. Secondly, the three ministers in charge of policy during the crisis – Robert Walpole, James Stanhope and Viscount Townshend – acted decisively and sensibly.[39] Thirdly, the Jacobites were badly let down by Providence, for Louis XIV, their greatest help in ages past, expired on 1 September 1715. Bolingbroke's despairing comment was: 'my hopes sank as he declined and died when he expired'. Louis had been on the throne for seventy-two years, so this was hardly an untimely death, but even a month or two more might have made a crucial difference, for he was deeply committed to the Jacobite cause for both personal and religious reasons.

He turned out to be the last French king to offer more than token support. As his successor, his great-grandson, was only five years old, everything now depended on the regent, the Duke of Orléans. If the infant Louis XV were to die, Orléans hoped to succeed to the French throne himself, but would face fierce competition from Louis XIV's grandson Philip V, King of Spain. In that contest, the support of the King of England would be very welcome. Another cogent argument was supplied by France's exhaustion after a generation of incessant and extremely expensive warfare. So orders went out to French ministers that the Jacobites were not to be assisted.[40]

That was probably the kiss of death, because – and this was the fourth reason – there simply was not enough support for the Pretender's cause in Britain to sustain a successful insurrection without French assistance. In the dream world of 'rumour, propaganda, fantasy, and illusion'[41] that made up the Jacobite mindset, 'the King over the water' was always on the point of making a triumphal entry to his capital, especially in the wishful thinking of two or three Tory squires when gathered together after hunting. But, if action as opposed to drinking toasts was required, wiser counsels prevailed. In the words of one despairing Jacobite: 'they are never right hearty for the cause, till they are mellow, as they call it, over a bottle or two, but they do not care for venturing their carcases any further than the tavern'.[42]

That was not the end of the Jacobites, of course. They lived on as a threat, not least because it was in the interest of the Whigs to exaggerate their menace and to tar every

Tory with the brush of treason. A Jacobite subculture continued to thrive in the clandestine press and clubs of London and in High Church rectories and manor houses across the country. It found public expression in the noisy celebrations mounted to mark certain anniversaries, especially 30 January (the execution of Charles I), 29 May (the restoration of Charles II) and 10 June (the Pretender's birthday). In 1718–19 the tragedy of 1715 was reprised as a farce, with a bizarre scheme initiated by Cardinal Alberoni, the Spanish first minister, in conjunction with the mercurial Charles XII of Sweden. Once again, it seemed that Providence was a Hanoverian Protestant. Firstly, King Charles was killed while besieging a Norwegian fortress (probably by one of his own side) and then, in March 1719, the Spanish invasion squadron, commanded by the ever-luckless Duke of Ormonde, was dispersed by a storm in the Bay of Biscay. Only around a thousand would-be insurgents eventually made it to Kintail on the north-west coast of Scotland, where the Spaniards surrendered and the Highlanders faded away into their inaccessible mountains and glens.[43]

It was on the Celtic periphery of the British Isles that resistance to the new monarch was naturally fiercest. Scotland was very different from England. It was much more rural, with only just over 5 per cent of the population living in towns of more than 10,000 (even Edinburgh had only 30,000 inhabitants); it was much poorer, its exports limited to raw materials; and it had no credible naval forces.[44] What prompted enough Scottish decision-makers to accept union with England in 1707 was the prospect of unfettered access to English domestic and colonial markets, this powerful economic argument strengthened by the liberal distribution of bribes and other favours. As the Act of Union incorporated the succession provisions of the Act of Settlement, it also guaranteed English assistance in preventing a Stuart restoration.[45] The Scots were given generous representation in Parliament, especially in the House of Commons, were allowed to keep their own legal system and laws and – most important of all for the great majority – the dominance of the Presbyterian Church was guaranteed.[46] Many agreed with William Carstares, Principal of Edinburgh University, that 'The desire I have to see our Church secured makes me in love with the Union as the most probable means to preserve it.'[47] Yet the union took a very long time to gain acceptance outside the charmed circle of its immediate beneficiaries. As Stanhope put it: 'Never did a treaty produce more ultimate advantage to a nation; never was any received with such general and thorough hatred.'[48] George was fortunate that the number of Scots appreciating the benefits of the union increased with every year that passed. Semiotic evidence of the Lowlands rallying to the new dynasty could be seen later in the century in street names – Hanover Street, George Street, Queen Street, Frederick Street.[49] There were enough unreconciled Catholics and Episcopalians to keep the threat of sedition alive, but – as the failed Jacobite rebellions of 1715 and 1719 showed – there were not enough of them to pose a serious threat. George appears to have taken little interest in his northern kingdom. He never went there and abolished the post of Secretary of State for Scotland established by the Act of Union. He did, however, direct that £20,000 of the income he derived from confiscated Jacobite estates should be spent on providing schools in the Highlands.[50]

Nor did Ireland engage his attention, his low opinion revealed by his ranking an English knighthood above an Irish peerage.[51] Like most of his English subjects, he appears to have regarded the country as a colony to be exploited: for example, he gave his German mistress Melusine the Irish coinage concession, which she promptly sold on to an unscrupulous entrepreneur, making a profit of £10,000 in the process.[52] In 1720 George gave his royal assent to the 'Declaratory Act', which both strengthened and made explicit English ascendancy. Entitled 'An Act for the better securing the dependency of the Kingdom of Ireland on the Crown of Great Britain', it asserted the right of the Westminster Parliament to legislate for Ireland 'in all cases whatever' and abolished the appellate jurisdiction of the Irish House of Lords in Irish matters. Even the English-born Protestant Bishop of Derry found this 'somewhat hard of digestion' and reported that 'a seditious spirit is arisen and grown rampant amongst us which is daily animating the populace to assert their Irish liberties'.[53] One brief flash of responsible rule came when George rejected as 'ridiculous' a proposal that Catholic priests caught proselytizing should be castrated.[54] In the event, there was no serious disturbance in Ireland during his reign, although the discrimination against Catholics, who made up 75 per cent of the population but owned only 14 per cent of the land, allowed a running sore to go on festering.

Paradoxically, whether dormant in Ireland or active in

Scotland, the Jacobites had done lucky George a good turn. Had there been no Catholic threat, his reception would have been even cooler than it actually was. A fifty-four-year-old German, physically unimpressive, without a trace of charisma, accompanied by an equally alien retinue, and with very little or no English was never going to find it easy to endear himself to his new subjects. Journalists of all stripes had a field day. One verse from *The Blessings attending George's accession* neatly sums up some of the more popular charges laid against him:

> Hither he brought the dear Illustrious House;
> That is, himself, his pipe, close stool and louse;
> Two Turks, three Whores, and half a dozen nurses,
> Five hundred Germans, all with empty purses.[55]

The 'two Turks' were Mohammed and Mustapha (spellings vary), originally prisoners of war. They were more like personal assistants than valets, for their duties went well beyond attending to his wardrobe and hygiene. Mohammed also looked after his personal accounts and acted as his gatekeeper. George clearly had a high opinion of them, preserving their images for posterity on the staircase fresco in Kensington Palace and securing a title of nobility for Mohammed from the Emperor Charles VI (as Georg Ludwig Maximilian Mohammed von Königstreu, which can be translated as 'Loyal to the King'). Such an unusual arrangement had tongues wagging about them being kept 'for abominable uses'.[56]

On the other hand, there was much malicious gossip about the two most prominent ladies in George's entourage – Melusine von der Schulenburg, nicknamed 'the Maypole' because she was tall and slim; and Sophia Charlotte von Kielmansegg, nicknamed 'the Elephant' because she was short and stout. The former had been George's mistress for more than two decades by the time she arrived in England, bearing him three daughters, all of whom accompanied their parents and were lodged at St James's Palace. Sophia Charlotte, however, was *not* George's mistress, as was generally asserted, but his half-sister, the illegitimate offspring of his father, Elector Ernst August.[57] George put her husband, Johann Adolf Baron von Kielmansegg, in charge of the royal stables, although he was barred from an official post by the Act of Settlement. The new arrivals benefited in other ways. Melusine became successively Duchess of Munster and Duchess of Kendal; Sophia Charlotte became Countess of Leinster and Countess of Darlington. They were also undoubtedly – and notoriously – venal, accepting bribes from all and sundry to influence George.[58] Given that George had divorced and then locked up his own wife for adultery, his seedy private life did nothing to burnish his image with a public that increasingly disapproved of sexual impropriety. This was the era of the Society for the Reformation of Manners (founded 1691), the Society for the Propagation of Christian Knowledge (1698) and the Society for the Propagation of the Gospel (1701). The dread 'English Sunday' antedated the Victorians by a century and more. As one caustic German observer remarked in 1710, sabbatarian observance provided the only indication that England was a Christian nation.[59]

In short, very few of George's new subjects were devoted to his person. They did not need to be. It was not what he was, but what he was not that mattered. He was not a Stuart, he was not a Catholic, and he was not a French puppet. So anyone contemplating the admittedly imperfect sovereign could reflect that he might be a lot worse. It is a point well made by Graham Gibbs: 'Whatever the blemishes of the Hanoverians, and they seemed numerous at the beginning of George I's reign, and continued to seem numerous under his successors, they seemed as dust in the balance compared with the awfulness of the Stuart alternative.'[60] So every Jacobite riot served to remind every British Protestant of the dangers of allowing disaffection to tip over into sedition. Well-publicized (and exaggerated) reports of Catholic oppression on the continent – the Heidelberg crisis of 1719 or the 'Thorn Massacre' in 1724, for example – helped to keep anti-papist paranoia alive.[61] Government-friendly newspapers made sure that George's credentials as Defender of the (Protestant) Faith were reinforced: 'His Majesty being determined to take all imaginable measures to redress the grievances of the oppress'd Protestants in the Empire, holds a Privy Council twice a week during his residence in Germany.'[62]

3
Court, Country and Family Matters

The new king came from a court which boasted a magnificent garden at Herrenhausen, but not much else. The modest electoral residence in downtown Hanover could not hold a candle to the palaces of most of George's fellow German princes. His new quarters were not so very different, except that there was no English equivalent of Herrenhausen. Indeed, the court lacked an architectural framework comparable with even a middling continental state. The main London palace, Whitehall, had been destroyed by a terrible fire in 1697, which had spared only Inigo Jones's Banqueting House, and had not been rebuilt. Everyone recognized the need for a new royal palace in the capital and many plans were drawn up, but nothing was actually done. St James's Palace, dating back to the reign of Henry VIII, was not an adequate replacement for Whitehall, consisting of a maze of small rooms. Daniel Defoe commented acidly: 'so far from having one single beauty to recommend it, 'tis at once the contempt of foreign nations and the disgrace of our own'.[1] Throughout George's reign there were commercial buildings piled up against its walls. They were eventually removed during the next reign, when the stench from a 'necessary house' belonging to a tavern became unbearable to its royal neighbours.[2]

Constrained by the tight limits imposed by the civil list and temperamentally averse to grand display, George was not a great builder. Only at Kensington Palace did he leave an enduring architectural mark. He vetoed Vanbrugh's plans for a great baroque replacement along the lines of Blenheim, ordering instead a modest reconstruction with two of the storeys completed 'in the cheapest and plainest manner' and 'such repairs as shall be found absolutely necessary (and no other)'.[3] With characteristic economy, to decorate the new rooms he commissioned William Kent instead of the better-known but much more expensive Sir James Thornhill. This proved to be a blessing in disguise. Thornhill already had the large spaces of the Painted Hall at Greenwich on which to display his baroque bravura, while Kent took the opportunity to move on to the more restrained classical style favoured by the circle of aesthetes led (and financed) by the Earl of Burlington from which he came. The decoration of the King's Grand Staircase has been rightly hailed as 'a masterpiece of mural art'. It is also unusual, presenting the portraits of forty-five court servants high and low, including such oddities as Ulrich Jorry, the Polish dwarf, and 'Peter the Wild Boy'. Just how much input came from the royal patron cannot be known, but it is certain that George liked Kent's creation 'very much' and approved 'of everything'.[4]

Although anything but extravagant, at the very start of his reign George was persuaded by Townshend to spend the large sum of £6,450 to buy the library of John Moore,

Bishop of Ely, the finest private collection of books in England. Even more remarkably, he at once gave it away, to the University of Cambridge, whose attachment to the Hanoverians differed sharply from the notoriously Jacobite enthusiasm of the University of Oxford. The gift inspired the following verse by the physician Sir William Browne:

> The King to Oxford sent a troop of horse,
> For Tories own no argument but force;
> With equal care to Cambridge books he sent,
> For Whigs allow no force but argument.[5]

Oxford did, however, also benefit from George's establishment of Regius Professorships of History at the two English universities in 1724. Alas, many years – decades – were to pass before either recipient turned this largesse to good use. In the meantime, the posts served primarily as additional sources of patronage to help keep the Whig oligarchy running smoothly. [6]

That was also the function of the court. The importance of a court to the efficient running of an early modern state is not in doubt.[7] It was the interface between ruler and elites. It was where the latter came for political influence, patronage, marriage partners and, last but not least, recreation. In the right hands – those of the young Louis XIV, for example – it could be a powerful weapon for the promotion of monarchical authority; in the wrong hands – those of the ageing Louis XIV and his successors, for example – it could become dysfunctional. George fell somewhere between the two. He got off to a bad start by confining his participation in court rituals to a minimum.

The ceremonial start to the day – the *lever* – he curtailed, preferring to be dressed, washed and shaved by Mohammed and Mustapha in the privacy of his bedroom. It was there also that he took his breakfast and spent the morning, reading despatches and other government papers. It was not until midday that he moved to his private study, or 'closet', a small room nearby reached by the back stairs, to receive by appointment ministers and other dignitaries.[8] However, he did condescend to appear regularly at 'Drawing Rooms', evening gatherings of the great and the good, where he played cards or stood at one end of the room conversing with anyone able to speak French.[9] His preferred form of relaxation, however, was private suppers with Melusine von der Schulenburg and their children, or visits to the theatre, also with his family, where he watched from a private box. Both formal occasions at court and appearances in public he avoided as much as possible.[10] On his return from Hanover in 1723, for example, orders were issued 'that there may be as little concourse of noisy attendants at his landing, or on the road to London as possible'.[11]

George had neither the means nor the wish to unfold grandiose representational displays of the kind favoured by so many of his fellow German princes. Back in Hanover, he had closed down the electoral opera company as soon as he succeeded his spendthrift father in 1698, although that was mainly due to the loss of the revenues from the bishopric of Osnabrück which had financed opera in the past.[12] In London, he was a frequent attender of the opera performances given by Johann Jakob Heidegger's company, contributing by paying a premium over and above the regular price of admission. It was not enough to save the enterprise, which collapsed in 1717. George was more forthcoming when its successor was established with the grand title 'The Royal Academy of Music', although his support was confined to a royal charter and an annual subsidy of £1,000. Despite its title, it was quite different from the continental court operas, being organized as a joint-stock company with the intention of making a profit. George continued as a regular attender for the rest of his life. The fact that during the first four months of 1727 he saw Handel's *Admeto* nineteen times allowed Donald Burrows to conclude that he 'was either a genuine lover of opera or a masochist'. In the course of his reign, and despite his six lengthy absences in Hanover, George attended fully half of all opera performances given in the capital. By advertising his enthusiasm, George probably did more to promote Handel's success than by his relatively modest financial support. In 1717 he was directly responsible for one of the most durable of all the composer's works. The *Daily Courant* reported that on 17 July George had enjoyed a river outing, travelling from Whitehall upriver to Chelsea in an open barge, accompanied by a second barge in which fifty instrumentalists 'of all sorts' played 'the finest Symphonies, compos'd express for this Occasion by Mr Handel; which his Majesty liked so well, that he caus'd it to be plaid over three times in going and returning'.[13] This became known as the *Water Music*.[14]

In only one other area that brought him into contact with his elites did George show real enthusiasm. That was hunting. To record that hunting was his 'passion' is to understate the case. Since time out of mind it had played a central role in the life of his Guelph ancestors, consuming huge amounts of time and money. Less than a year before her death, George's eighty-three-year-old mother wrote to her daughter, the Queen of Prussia, that she had just got back from 'a very fine hunt' at which she had been in at the death.[15] The Hanoverians were fortunate that their lands included some of the best hunting grounds in Europe. Especially in the great oak and beech forests to the west of the River Elbe, game of all kinds teemed on a reserve covering more than 5,000 hectares.[16] At Göhrde, its centre, George transformed the existing hunting lodge into a true palace, his most ambitious and expensive building project. It was here that his court came for two or three months every autumn.[17] By the time he had finished in 1712, topping off his work with a splendid theatre, the complex comprised twenty-three buildings with stables for more than 150 horses and kennels for more than 400 hounds (most of them English-bred stag hounds and greyhounds).[18] When he reached England, he must have been relieved to find that his enthusiasm was shared by most peers and landed gentry and that an extensive hunting establishment was at his disposal. He made full use of the opportunities offered by the forests around Hampton Court and Windsor, combining a day in the field with visits to the country seats of the local Whig grandees.[19] Nor was hunting confined to its traditional supporters, for the royal buckhounds were also followed by City merchants and financiers, professional men and even Anglican prelates.[20] Just how much their common pursuit of the stag helped to bond the king with his elites cannot be assessed, but may have helped to demonstrate that when it came to the really important things in life, he was not so alien after all.

In general, however, George made little attempt to adjust from absolutist elector to parliamentary monarch. Aloof, taciturn, perhaps shy, he simply lacked the personality to make his court work as it should. This reticence was not sensible. In a parliamentary monarchy such as the British, with a large and rapidly growing public sphere, the sovereign who neglected public relations made life more difficult than it needed to be. Ironically, it took a vicious family quarrel to persuade George to become sociable. There is no way of knowing when he began to take exception to his eldest son and heir, Georg August, whom he was obliged to make the Prince of Wales on his arrival in England. Against the attractive notion that he had always hated him as the child of his detested ex-wife is the knowledge that he treated the daughter of that ill-starred marriage with patently genuine affection.[21] Perhaps it was having to live in such close proximity in the cramped quarters of St James's Palace that set his teeth on edge. Perhaps it was the knowledge that, as he was an elderly man by the standards of the day, it would probably not be long before the grim reaper forced him to make way for his impatient heir apparent. Relations between rulers and their eldest sons were notoriously fraught. At least George did not follow the example of Peter the Great of Russia, who had the Tsarevich Alexei tortured to death, or the rather less extreme example of Frederick William I of

Prussia, who systematically abused Crown Prince Frederick both physically and psychologically.

What was probably long-incubating mutual hostility came into the open in 1716 when George returned to Hanover. As the Jacobite rebellion had only just been suppressed, the English ministers tried to persuade him not to go. He was adamant, his eagerness to return to the land of his birth (and the hunting at Göhrde) not exactly flattering to his new subjects. He was also adamant that the Prince of Wales should not act as a fully fledged viceroy in his absence and forbade him to make appointments or take policy decisions.[22] Also offensive was his insistence that the prince's senior aide, the Duke of Argyll, be dismissed from his service. As the duke was already nursing a grievance over being removed from his military command, this guaranteed that one of the most influential Whig grandees would go into opposition. The Prince of Wales retaliated in two ways. Firstly, in his father's absence he organized lavish court festivities, entertained on a grand scale, dined in public, went on a royal progress through the home counties to Portsmouth, paraded his knowledge of the English language and generally showed how a king of England ought to behave towards his elites. That he was always accompanied by his intelligent, comely and congenial wife Caroline only served to emphasize the contrast with the gloomy ambience of his father's entourage.[23] Secondly, he encouraged – or at least did nothing to prevent – the formation of a 'reversionary interest', that is to say the alternative centre of political identity that always developed around an heir apparent, especially when the incumbent was elderly. As the Victorian Whig historian Henry Hallam sagely observed: 'from unknown princes men are prone to hope much'.[24]

King George was in no hurry to return from his electorate, staying on beyond the end of the hunting season and into the winter of 1716–17. Needless to say, there was no shortage of courtiers encouraging him to think the worst of what was going on back in London. They were led by the ambitious and unscrupulous Earl of Sunderland, who insinuated to George that his son and daughter-in-law were ingratiating themselves with the British public at his expense and building their own political party.[25] When George got back to England in January 1717, battle commenced. By May, the Prince of Wales was being referred to as 'the leader of the opposition', as he gathered around him dissident Whigs and even Tories. His father responded by preventing him from dining in public but also excluding him and his wife from the royal table.[26] More subtly, by raising his game at court he showed that a king had the resources to outshine a mere Prince of Wales. The surly recluse metamorphosed into a gorgeous baroque peacock. During the three summer months at Hampton Court, on every Thursday and Sunday there were lavish dinners for up to fifty of those he wished to woo. Every day he made himself available to his courtiers, dining with them, walking with them, playing cards with them. There were special 'ladies' days' and a reception every evening. In short, he was now behaving in the regal manner expected by his subjects.[27] When he learned in the autumn that his detested son proposed to go to Newmarket for the racing, he 'took the sudden resolution of being present at the diversions of that place', as the Secretary of State, Joseph Addison, recorded.[28] The boating expedition which yielded Handel's *Water Music* may well have been part of this campaign.

This 'battle of the courts' proved to be just the prelude for the major eruption that occurred on 28 November 1717. The occasion was the christening of the Wales's new-born son. The parents had wanted George's brother, Ernst August, the Prince Bishop of Osnabrück, to stand as god-father, but the British ministers persuaded the king that tradition required the Lord Chamberlain, the Duke of Newcastle, to serve. Although the Prince of Wales com-plied with a royal directive to this effect, when leaving the ceremony he turned to Newcastle and hissed, 'Rascal, I find you out!' Unfortunately, what Newcastle thought he said was 'Rascal, I fight you out!' Naturally timorous, he rushed off to seek royal protection against the prospect of a duel with the heir to the throne. George now exploded, as months and possibly years of hatred boiled over, and he at once ordered his son's arrest. He called off the yeomen of the guard only when reminded that under English law a writ of habeas corpus prevented arbitrary imprisonment, even when commanded by the sovereign.[29]

The royal family was now at war, setting a pattern that was to be followed by each succeeding generation of Hano-verians, at least until the twentieth century. The Prince of Wales was banished from St James's Palace, moving first to rented accommodation in Albemarle Street and then to Leicester House in the eponymous square. His wife Caro-line followed him into exile, although George had wanted her to stay at the palace, her charm and beauty more than compensating for her sharp tongue and intimidating intellect. But their three little daughters, aged seven, five and three, were not allowed to go with their parents, nor was their baby brother, the unwitting cause of the rupture. Although the death of the infant prince three months later could not have been prevented, George's breaking up of the family is difficult to excuse. It does not seem to have been dictated by a grandparent's doting devotion, for when the eldest of the three girls, Princess Anne, was asked whether the king ever came to visit them, she replied, 'Oh no, he does not love us enough for that.'[30] On learning that the parents had been making clandestine visits to the royal nursery, George at once intervened.[31] It was a sad reprise of the cruelty he had shown back in 1694 when he directed that his divorced wife should never be allowed to see their children (then aged seven and ten) again.

For the next three years, this unedifying spectacle continued. At least it kept the king up to the mark at court and the ill wind blew money to those who served its manifold needs. In August 1718, for example, the rumour that the Prince of Wales was about to open a theatre at his summer residence at Richmond and was recruiting a company of actors prompted George to order at once that a rival stage be erected in the Great Hall at Hampton Court and a leading troupe (Steele's) be summoned to perform on it.[32] A more permanent social weapon were the 'Drawing Rooms' held three times a week, with George doing his best to be affable. In addition, more ambitious events involving music and dancing were held on a regular basis at Kensington

Palace, to which the court moved in the summer. According to one report from there, 'the ladies say they never see so much company and every body fine, the King very obliging and in great good humour . . . all the garden illuminated and music and dancing in the Green House and the long Gallery'.[33]

4
Whigs and Tories

Overlapping the family altercation – and helping to intensify it – was a party-political clash, or rather an *intra*-party-political clash, for George's accession had turned the country into something approaching a one-party state. As we have seen, on arrival he had signalled a willingness to accommodate the Tories but had been rebuffed. The subsequent treason of Bolingbroke and Ormonde misled him into believing those Whigs who were assuring him that *all* Tories were Jacobites.[1] In reality, most were either supporters of the Hanoverian succession or fence-sitters, getting off on the Hanoverian side when the abject failure of the 'Fifteen' made it clear that George had come to stay. It was a bad time to be a Tory. Intense government pressure had ensured that the general election of 1715 turned a very large Tory majority into a rather less large Whig majority.[2] Dismissed from their lucrative positions in central government, purged from the localities, abandoned by their leaders, they could only wail and gnash their teeth in the wilderness. Bolingbroke wrote to Jonathan Swift from his French exile in October 1716: 'they are got into a dark hole, where they grope about after blind guides, stumble from mistake to mistake, jostle against one another and dash their heads against the wall, and all this to no purpose. For assure yourself, that there is no returning to light.'[3]

Worse was to come. The gleeful Whigs took full advantage of their power to dismantle the High Church legislation enacted by the previous ministry. The mirror image of the Jacobite smear applied to the Tories was the allegation voiced by High Church Tories that there was not 'a single Whig who is not a professed deist and enemy to all religion, a Latitudinarian, or notoriously opposed to the Church of England', as the arch-Jacobite Bishop Francis Atterbury put it in a pamphlet of 1714.[4] That was equally untrue. If every Nonconformist, deist or free-thinker was almost certain not to be Tory (the unbelieving Bolingbroke being the exception that proved the rule), the great majority of Whigs were Anglican Christians. Where they differed was in their attitude to religious pluralism. That had been demonstrated by the case of Dr Henry Sacheverell, put on trial in 1710 for preaching a High Church sermon that sailed very close to a Jacobite wind. His creed of passive obedience, non-resistance, no toleration of non-Anglicans, closure of dissenting academies, an end to occasional conformity (the practice of taking Communion according to the Anglican rite once a year just to qualify for office) and any form of accommodation with Nonconformists, was hugely popular. His virtual acquittal (the sentence was a mere suspension from office for three years) was greeted with wild acclamation by both Tory grandees and plebeians, but it turned out to be the high-water mark of his brand of churchmanship. The Acts against occasional conformity and dissenting schools passed in the summer of

1714 were due to come into effect on the very day that Queen Anne died. At his very first Privy Council meeting, the new king made a programmatic statement in favour of toleration and religious pluralism by announcing that he wanted both Acts repealed.[5] Although that was not accomplished until January 1719, in the interim they had been a dead letter. George would also have liked to see the repeal of the Test and Corporation Acts, which confined public office to Anglicans, but not enough support could be mustered to get it through Parliament. Even so, the new reign marked a turning point in the religious history of England and it was one for which George could claim some credit. If Queen Anne had lived longer – and she was only forty-nine when she died – things might have been very different. Shortly after her death, a delegation of Nonconformists led by the famous Independent minister Thomas Bradbury went to court to present their congratulations to the new sovereign. There they bumped into Bolingbroke, who took one look at their sombre black gowns and asked them derisively whether they were going to a funeral. 'Yes, My Lord,' cried Bradbury exultantly, 'it is the funeral of the Schism Act, and the resurrection of liberty!'[6]

George was Supreme Head of the Church of England and he made his powers of patronage count. One of Queen Anne's last ecclesiastical appointments was to appoint the Jacobite Francis Atterbury Bishop of Rochester (although she did it through gritted teeth); one of George's first was to make the vigorous Whig polemicist Benjamin Hoadly Bishop of Bangor. When the Low Church Whig Edmund Gibson became Bishop of London in 1723, the way was clear to complete the remodelling of the English episcopate, for nine sees fell vacant in that year and in each case the royal choice followed his recommendation.[7] The other side of the coin was the fate of Atterbury, on whose advice the Schism Bill against dissenting academies had been introduced in 1714. In 1722 he very foolishly allowed himself to be drawn into a harebrained Jacobite plot involving, as usual, the incorrigible Duke of Ormonde.[8] Charged with high treason and sent to the Tower, he was allowed to escape with his life but was sent across the Channel into permanent banishment. In G. V. Bennett's assessment, this 'was a turning-point in British politics and a decisive blow to the Tory cause'. Even the Pretender – by now safely removed to Rome – had to concede that there was no support in England for his cause (except perhaps on some Oxford high tables).[9] Henry Sacheverell died in 1724 and was buried in the churchyard of St Andrew's, Holborn, next to the grave of Sally Salisbury, the most famous prostitute of her day, a coincidence which inspired the epitaph: 'A fit companion for a High Church priest / He non-resistance taught, and she profest.'[10]

Arguments about the apostolic succession or the Eucharist threw only a light veil over political issues. It seems reasonable to conclude that the Prince of Wales's support for the bishops opposing the repeal of the Occasional Conformity or Schism Acts was motivated more by a desire to annoy his father than by any concern for religious truth. Also to the fore in opposing any concessions to Nonconformists was the arch-Whig Sir Robert Walpole, who 'bore harder against the Court than any Tory durst attempt to do'.[11] The reason for this hypocrisy was obvious to all – Walpole was out of office and was trying to make such a nuisance of himself that he would have be taken in again. His fluctuating relationship with George illustrated how both men had to undergo a prolonged political education before achieving a stable and mutually beneficial rapport.

When George arrived in England he was lucky to find a new generation of able politicians willing to do his business. The old guard of Whigs conveniently died off – the Marquis of Wharton and the Earl of Halifax in the spring of 1715 and Lord Somers a year later. They made room for four men of exceptional talent and ambition – the Earl of Sunderland (aged thirty-nine), James Stanhope (forty-two), Viscount Townshend (forty) and Robert Walpole (thirty-eight). Politicians being what they were – and are – Westminster proved to be not big enough for all four of them. Once the Tories had been seen off to the shires, or at least the back benches, the Whig leaders naturally conspired against each other. Initially, the dominant figure was Townshend, whom George made Secretary of State for the Northern Department. His brother-in-law Walpole was assigned only the junior, if highly lucrative, office of Paymaster General. As he was Marlborough's son-in-law, Sunderland had expected a plum but was given a prickly pear in the shape of the Lord Lieutenancy of Ireland and at once deployed his impressive conspiratorial skills to achieve a promotion. His chance came when George went off to Hanover in the summer of 1716, accompanied by Stanhope, the Secretary of State for the Southern Department. Pleading the need to restore his health, Sunderland

set off to take the waters at Aachen but soon moved further north-east to Hanover. As we have seen, he then
persuaded George that the Prince and Princess of Wales
were usurping his regal position by building an alternative
centre of power and he also implicated Townshend and
Walpole, who were back in London and ignorant of what
was going on at Hanover.

There was actually some substance to the rift that now
opened up between the two ministers in London and the
two at Hanover. As we shall see in the next chapter,
George, Sunderland and Stanhope were eager to sign the
triple alliance with the French and Dutch that they had
negotiated in secret with the Duke of Orléans's envoy,
Dubois. Townshend and Walpole were opposed, conclud-
ing, not without reason, that the Hanoverian tail was
being allowed to wag the British dog.[12] George was not
used to being obstructed by his servants and did not like it.
Limited the British monarchy may have been, but the king
still exercised considerable powers, notably the right to
appoint his ministers and control the armed forces. Given
his Hanoverian and military background, it was not sur-
prising that George liked to command and dealt swiftly
with overt disobedience. So in December 1716 Townshend
was demoted to the Lord Lieutenancy of Ireland (the Siber-
ia of English politicians) and finally dismissed altogether
in April 1717. Walpole joined him in opposition.

The two friends had fatally underestimated Sunderland,
unaware that he had won over both the king and Stanhope. As so often in politics, it was proximity to power
that had proved decisive. So from the spring of 1717

George was served by a ministry led by Sunderland as Secretary of State and Stanhope as First Lord of the Treasury and Chancellor of the Exchequer. As the latter's expertise lay mainly in foreign affairs, after a year the two men exchanged offices. Stanhope was always George's favourite minister, thanks to his military background, cosmopolitan experience, good knowledge of French and compliant personality.[13] His reward was to be made a baron and viscount in 1717 and an earl less than a year later. His sudden death from a stroke in February 1721 affected George deeply: 'His Majesty was so sensibly touch'd that he could not eat his supper, and retired for two hours into his Closet to lament the loss of such an able statesman and Faithfull Counsellor and so loyal a subject.' Stanhope was given a grand funeral with full military honours, attended by the king and the Prince of Wales, the hearse escorted by '200 Horse-Grenadiers, 200 Life Guards, 2 battalions of Foot Guards, all officers being in cypress mourning, scarfs and hatbands'.[14]

During the last few months of his life, Stanhope's political authority had been diluted by the need to readmit Townshend and Walpole to government. He and Sunderland had been forced to make this concession by three interwoven considerations. The first was the friction caused by the presence of Hanoverian ministers in London. As George continued to rule a large and important state of the Holy Roman Empire, it was natural that he should bring and retain officials to deal with its affairs. They were assigned two offices, which became known as the 'German Chancery', in St James's Palace. Of the four important

enough to acquire political significance, the least prominent was Johann Philipp von Hattorf, who was responsible
for the day-to-day running of the office and specialized in
military affairs.[15] Next came the shadowy but influential
figure of Jean de Robethon, a Huguenot who left France in
1685 and had served William III and then Georg Wilhelm
of Celle, before becoming Georg Ludwig's private secretary in 1705.[16] Once he reached London in 1714, he used
his proximity to the new king to support the Whigs, especially Stanhope and Sunderland, and to make money from
influencing appointments.[17]

A more public figure was Hans Kaspar Count von Bothmer, a long-serving Hanoverian diplomat who was in
London when Queen Anne died and played an important
part in expediting the change of dynasty.[18] He stayed on
in London, his ready access to the new king encouraging
suspicions that British foreign policy was being run by
Germans.[19] Also in the firing line was Baron Andreas Got-
tlieb von Bernstorff, George's senior Hanoverian minister.
A more assertive figure than his other colleagues, he had
given an early indication of his taste for adventure with a
high-risk liaison with the wife of his prince and first
employer, the Duke of Mecklenburg.[20] In one more cheer-
ing illustration of the pluralism allowed by the territorial
fragmentation of the Holy Roman Empire, he had not only
escaped punishment but had been able to move a few miles
west and join Guelph service. There he served first Georg
Wilhelm of Celle and then Georg Ludwig of Hanover,
becoming his first minister in 1709. Although the influence
of this 'Hanoverian Junto' was of course talked up

by Tories and opposition Whigs, there was enough sub-stance in the charge to elevate it beyond rumour. It was suspected, for example, that Bernstorff's attitude to Prus-sia was soured by a dispute over feudal rights on one of his estates.[21]

The influence of these Hanoverians was naturally great-est during the early part of the reign. Apart from one brief visit back in 1680, George had no experience and little knowledge of England. Robethon and Bothmer had both. But as their master gained in confidence, came to know and trust at least some of his English ministers, and per-haps even began to see himself as representing British interests, the Junto's dominance waned. On the other side, the English ministers themselves began to resent the Hano-verians' intervention in matters that did not concern them. As we have seen, Townshend and Walpole resigned rather than submit. Sunderland and Stanhope soldiered on but eventually they too revolted. Matters came to a head in July 1719 over the Prussian alliance. When George opted for it, he also opted for Stanhope over Bernstorff. 'We have at last got a complete victory over the old man', crowed the former about the latter in July.[22] He was right. This was an important moment in George's reign. When he told his Hanoverian ministers that they were not even to speak to him about English matters, he was also announcing that he was now first and foremost King of England. Bernstorff went back to Hanover with him in 1720 and did not return. Bothmer stayed on in London, living in a house that was later to be called '10 Downing Street' until his death in 1732, despite the 'the ruinous Condition of the

Premises' about which he repeatedly complained.[23] Always less assertive than Bernstorff, he now heeded his master's command and confined himself to strictly Hanoverian business.

A common desire to cut the Hanoverians down to size paved the way for a rapprochement between the two Whig factions. It was helped along by Sunderland and Stanhope's failure to get through Parliament a legislative programme which included the emasculation of the Test and Corporation Acts, relief for Roman Catholics, reform of the universities, repeal of the Septennial Act and, most importantly, the peerage bill.[24] The last-named would have fixed the membership of the House of Lords and allowed new creations only if a peer died without heirs. Leading the opposition in the House of Commons was Walpole, whose fabled eloquence inflicted on the government a crushing defeat. In one authoritative assessment, it was the best speech he ever made, which is saying a great deal. Even an opponent had to concede that it 'had as much of natural eloquence and of genius in it as had been heard by any of the audience within those walls'.[25] Once again, the independent country members had shown that royal support for ministers was not always enough to win a majority for the government. George, Stanhope and Sunderland needed no further proof that Walpole had to be brought back in.

Walpole was prepared to accept a subordinate post – the Paymaster Generalship, his old cash cow – and so was Townshend, who was to become Lord President of the Council, but they did insist that George should bring to an end the feud with his heir. As it happened, Walpole was just the man to orchestrate a reconciliation, for he had fostered good relations with the two influential ladies on either side. The first was George's mistress Melusine von der Schulenburg, recently elevated to be Duchess of Kendal. Walpole told Lord Cowper that 'her Interest did Everything; that she was, in effect as much Queen of England as ever any was; that he did Everything by her'. That comment was recorded by Cowper's wife, whose diary provides a detailed account of the intense negotiations between representatives of the warring parties in April 1720.[26] As she and her husband were part of the Wales's intimate circle, it is a particularly valuable source. Although physically unimpressive, Walpole knew how to ingratiate himself with women. An even more important ally was the Princess of Wales, whom 'Walpole has engrossed and monopolised . . . to a Degree of making her deaf to Everything that did not come from him', or so Lady Cowper claimed.[27] With two such headstrong and obstinate men involved, the intermediary's task was not an easy one. It was not until 23 April, coincidentally St George's Day, that the two Georges made up. That both did so with truculent ill grace did not matter. When Lady Cowper went to St James's Palace at five in the afternoon, she found 'the Square full of Coaches; the Rooms full of Company; Everything gay and laughing; Nothing but kissing and wishing of Joy'. Out on the streets, there was 'Hallooing and all Marks of Joy which could be shown by the Multitude'.[28]

Almost everyone benefited. The prince and princess could return to court and see their children again. The king had the accumulated civil list debt of £600,000 paid off and could enjoy a return to parliamentary tranquillity. Walpole and Townshend could clamber back on board the gravy train, albeit to the restaurant car rather than the driver's cab. The greatest losers, apart from a number of placemen dismissed to make room for opposition Whigs coming in from the cold, were the Hanoverian ministers, who had been kept completely in the dark. When Stanhope rather spitefully broke the news to Bernstorff and Bothmer at court 'in his shrill Scream', they were thunderstruck. Bothmer 'could not bear the Insult, nor the being given up by his old master, and burst into Tears'.[29] Another casualty was the profligate court George had maintained to out-shine his son. Probably breathing a sigh of relief, George reverted to his earlier pattern of behaviour. The 'Drawing Rooms' could not be dropped, but the lavish dining, music, dancing and theatricals were scaled back.[30] He now urged foreign governments to send ministers rather than full ambassadors, to avoid the elaborate ceremonial which reception of the latter involved.[31]

Walpole rejoined the government in June 1720, just in time to save George from the fallout from 'the most dramatic financial storm in eighteenth-century England'.[32] This was the 'South Sea Bubble'. The story began in 1711 when the South Sea Company was created as a Tory rival to the Whig Bank of England, with the specific objective of exchanging £9,000,000 of the National Debt for company stock. Although assigned the right to trade with Spanish America acquired at the Peace of Utrecht in 1713, commerce took second place to financial dealing.

On 7 April 1720, or in other words a couple of weeks before the rapprochement just related, royal assent was given to an Act of Parliament allowing the company to increase its capital by £30,000,000. This was believed to be sufficient to complete the conversion of the National Debt. The result was a sequence of events that began as a comedy, quickly degenerated into farce and ended as tragedy, as Peter Dickson put it.[33] In the process, a colossal amount of money was made and even more money was lost. £100 of stock had risen to £320 by mid April, £700 by June before reaching a peak of £1,050 before falling back to £950 in July, £800 in August, £300 by the end of September and £200 by the end of October.[34] The nimble minority made a fortune, the great majority lost their shirts.

The victims included not just City financiers but the needy and the greedy from all walks of life and every part of the country. Of course they looked for guilty men to punish and they did not have far to search. Not only parliamentary palms had been greased to get the legislation through, the corruption went right to the top. The Duchess of Kendal had received £15,000 of company stock on the (correct) assumption that she would recommend the scheme to her royal bedfellow; their two younger daughters received £5,000 worth each.[35] George himself had cannily quintupled his money, buying a first subscription of £20,000 and selling it for £106,400.[36] None of this could be kept secret and the stories grew with the telling. The dynasty wobbled. It was not only Jacobites who believed that if the Pretender had chosen this moment to appear in England, he would have met little resistance.[37]

Luckily for George, Walpole was on hand to save him. Although he did dabble in South Sea stock, not very successfully, he had played no part in the preparation of the legislation and did not join the government until after it had become law. Untainted by association with the band of knaves and fools who had inflated the Bubble, in the course of the winter of 1720–21 he devised a rescue package which drew some of the sting of angry investors and restored stability to the markets.[38] Perhaps more important were his repeated interventions in Parliament to shelter the king's servants from the wrath of the dispossessed, earning him the ironic but admiring nickname 'The Skreen-Master General'. The directors of the South Sea Company were thrown to the wolves, their great estates confiscated and sold, but, of the politicians, only the Chancellor of the Exchequer, John Aislabie, was punished severely. A huge slice of luck for Walpole was Stanhope's death. Not only did this put a convenient scapegoat out of reach, it also removed one of the two ministers senior to Walpole in George's pecking order. The other was Sunderland, whom Walpole dealt with ingeniously by smothering him with kindness. It was thanks to another of his bravura performances in the House of Commons that Sunderland escaped censure. Walpole got the best of both worlds: the gratitude of the king for saving his first minister, but the removal from office of a rival too damaged to continue. The way was now clear for him gradually to become so undisputedly the leader of the ministry as to earn the sobriquet 'the first British Prime Minister'.

This did not happen overnight. Townshend remained an equally prominent figure in the government; indeed there is evidence that George preferred him, making his son Horatio a peer in 1723 and himself a Knight of the Garter in 1724. For this latter honour Walpole had to wait until 1726. Relations between the two men began to fray once they were back in power. The death of Dolly, Walpole's sister and Townshend's wife, from smallpox in March 1726 severed the last thread, although it was not until the next reign that Townshend returned to Norfolk to devote himself full-time to agricultural improvement and acquire the title 'Turnip Townshend'.[39] Walpole also saw off a challenge from the younger generation in the attractive shape of John, Lord Carteret, who commended himself to George by his charm and amazing (for an Englishman) linguistic skills, including an ability to converse in fluent German. A successful diplomatic mission to Sweden in 1719–20 (of which more below) confirmed him as the coming man and he was made Secretary of State for the Southern Department in 1721 at the age of thirty. Alas, his brilliance was not supported by the more mundane qualities necessary for survival in the Westminster jungle. As Lord Hervey commented, he was 'marvellous . . . in spirit and in words', but 'a man that almost every body commends and no body is a friend to'.[40] Outmanoeuvred by Walpole, he was sent off to be Lord Lieutenant of Ireland in 1724.

As we have seen, George was very lucky to find so many able politicians to do his work. Not surprisingly, it took him some time to adjust to the very different pace of political life in London. The lesson he learned was that, although he undoubtedly had the right to choose his ministers, he could not keep them in office if they lost control of the House of Commons. That was how Walpole came to the top of the heap, and that was why he refused promotion to the House of Lords – at least until he eventually fell from power in 1742. There was more to this, however, than his wonderful ability to work the patronage system and dazzle the country members with his oratory. In an exceptionally penetrating passage in his great work *The Financial Revolution in England*, Peter Dickson identified Walpole's essential contribution to the success of the reign of George I (and of the Hanoverians who followed him). Walpole saw that England's victory in the wars of 1688–1713 stemmed from a de facto alliance between the landed and the monied interests. Through Parliament, the former voted the huge taxes and loans needed for military and naval success. Through the City of London, the latter provided the expertise necessary to sustain a war effort out of all proportion to the country's relatively modest population. Each resented the other, but each needed the other. It was Walpole's insight that he must allow all to feel that the government fundamentally represented their interest, however much they might criticize individual measures. So he kept the land tax low and did not pursue Stanhope's more ambitious schemes for Nonconformist emancipation, but he also passed acts of indemnity to protect religious dissenters and cultivated good relations with the great merchants and financiers of the City.[41] Against this judicious alliance, even Tories as eloquent as Bolingbroke railed in vain. In any case, their assumption of a radical division between old and new forms of wealth was increasingly out of date, as monied men bought land and landowners invested in commerce. Nor could Parliament be accused of being representative only of land, for over a hundred parliamentary boroughs were ports or fishing towns.[42]

5

The Sinews of Power and Foreign Policy

George came from an electorate whose economy was modestly prosperous but torpid. In England he encountered a dynamic kingdom well on the way to becoming the workshop and counting-house of the world. When Daniel Defoe made his tour through England and Scotland, beginning in 1722, he was aware that he was travelling through a single national economy. Unlike in almost every other European country, there were no internal customs barriers. The tax imposed on coal brought to London from the north-east to finance the building of St Paul's Cathedral was the exception that proved the rule. On leaving London in 1706, the Venetian ambassador gave this customs union the credit for putting English industry in advance of the rest of Europe.[1] It was also an economy united by excellent communications, for no part of Great Britain is more than 70 miles from the coast, a natural asset supplemented by more than 1,000 miles of navigable rivers. The fact that none of the cereal-growing regions were more than two days' journey away from access to water transport made local agricultural and horticultural specialization possible, with corresponding benefits for productivity.[2] If most roads turned into glutinous mud pits when it rained, the rapid expansion after 1695 of turnpikes (which upgraded road services in return for a toll), to reach a network of about 11,000 miles by the middle of the next century, made travel and transport quicker and cheaper.[3] In short, man and nature combined to create a national market, in marked contrast to England's nearest neighbour and chief rival France, memorably described by David Landes as 'a mosaic of semi-autarkic cells'.[4]

The population of England, Wales and Scotland was just short of 7,000,000 in 1714, a total that could easily be fed from local resources. England in particular had been a grain-exporting country since the 1670s and became a heavy exporter after 1714.[5] Although there were good years and bad years, all the economic indicators pointed upwards, revealing increases in productivity, income, life expectancy and both physical and social mobility. Between 1700 and 1731 exports went up by 17 per cent and imports by 27 per cent. An involuntary contribution to this growing prosperity was made by the very large numbers of slaves transported across the Atlantic in British ships. In the course of the 1720s alone 211,000 were delivered, to which terrible total another 32,000 who died en route must be added. During the first quarter of the eighteenth century, the industrial economy expanded by 15 per cent, agriculture by about the same amount, overseas trade by 30 per cent, but population by only 9 per cent. A visible increase in prosperity was the result, expressed in many complacent observations. Even before the War of the Spanish Succession had set the seal on British expansion, Defoe had hailed England as the most '*Diligent* Nation in the World, vast Trade, Rich Manufactures, mighty Wealth, universal Correspondence and happy Success has been constant Companions of *England*, and given us the Title of an Industrious People, and so in general we are'. In *A General Treatise of Husbandry and Gardening*, published in 1724, Richard Bradley proclaimed: 'The Improvement of Land, and the Study of Agriculture, have greatly contributed to render our Nation famous above all other Countries.'[6] In short, this relatively favourable economic background made a major contribution to the success of the new dynasty.[7]

George's good fortune extended to the exploitation of these burgeoning riches. By 1714 Britain boasted a sophisticated system of public credit and an efficient tax-gathering system. Although the origins of what has rightly been called a 'financial revolution' stretched back deep into the seventeenth century, it was the arrival of William III in 1688 that initiated the decisive phase. He brought with him Dutch ideas and a Dutch war. The cost of the first two phases of this 'Second Hundred Years War' – the Nine Years War of 1688–97 and the War of the Spanish Succession of 1701–13 – was on a scale never before experienced in English history. The first cost three times as much as Charles II's war against the Dutch of the 1660s, the second five times as much.[8] The national debt stood at zero in 1688; ten years of war ran it up to £17,300,000; and by 1714 it had reached £36,200,000. To manage borrowing on this unprecedented scale, the Bank of England was established in 1694, modelled on the Bank of Amsterdam.

That it would be a success was signalled right from the start when the original subscription was filled 'with almost contemptuous ease' in ten days, the king and queen heading the lists.[9] In 1706 the Lord Treasurer, Godolphin, observed smugly that, while England could borrow all the money it needed at 4–5 per cent, Louis XIV had to pay five times that rate.[10] It was a comparison which revealed the superior viability of a parliamentary monarchy: a loan to the English Treasury was guaranteed by Parliament, whose collateral was the total landed wealth of the kingdom; a loan to the King of France was a loan to an individual without any comparable institutional backing, an act of faith rather than a rational investment. By 1712 his credit was exhausted and French finances were 'on the verge of complete and utter collapse'.[11]

As important as loans were taxes. Here too the superior legitimacy conveyed by a parliamentary regime made for efficiency. It was Parliament which approved taxation and it was Parliament's Commissioners of Public Accounts who scrutinized public income and expenditure. Out in the shires, it was the MPs and their country gentry colleagues who sat on the county land tax commissions to ensure fair play.[12] In fact it was often *un*fair, as the actual as opposed to the nominal rate varied appreciably from one part of the country to another, but it was transparent and 'exemplified the engagement of key social groups in the country in the fiscal and political process'.[13] Moreover, as it had to be voted anew every year, it also guaranteed regular meetings of Parliament. As Martin Daunton has convincingly argued, the secret of an efficient taxation system is trust: 'taxpayers have little incentive to pay their taxes in the absence of a high degree of "trust" that other taxpayers and the government were fulfilling their obligations'.[14] Unlike in France, there were no aristocratic or clerical exemptions and no grandiloquent court culture to destroy trust. On the other hand, there was a real and growing problem of corruption in public life. Everyone knew, or pretended to know, that the wheels of government were lubricated by favours, bribes, perks and kickbacks. A central question, especially for those out of office, was: is parliamentary sovereignty possible without parliamentary corruption?[15] Once Walpole and the Whig oligarchs had consolidated their hold on power, this was to become a major issue, fuelling the 'patriot' opposition that was to cause George II so many problems. For the time being, despite the malodorous South Sea Bubble affair, parliamentary control seemed to be a sufficient safeguard.

Direct taxation on land was popular with parliamentarians because it was Parliament that controlled it. Beyond their reach but increasingly important was the revenue generated by customs and excise, whose share rose from two-thirds to three-quarters during the first half of the eighteenth century. The advantages of these forms of indirect taxation were twofold. Firstly, although they were 'socially regressive', bearing heaviest on the poor because they were taxes on consumption, the fact that they were paid at the port of entry or in the manufactory and were included in the price meant that they were relatively 'invisible'. Secondly, they allowed the state to benefit from the expansion of commerce, through customs dues, and from the consumer revolution that was passing excisable commodities such as tea, sugar and tobacco down the social scale to become the necessities of the masses rather than the luxuries of the rich. After 1660 the outsourcing of collection to tax farmers was gradually abandoned. Instead, there developed a network of professionally trained and centrally supervised state employees, whose numbers rapidly increased as the demands of warfare increased. By the time George reached England, there were 1,750 customs officers (a rise of a third since 1690) and 2,247 excise men (up 85 per cent).[16] To use a term made popular by John Brewer, this represented the creation of a 'fiscal-military state': 'dependent upon a complex system of measurement and book-keeping, organised as a rigorous hierarchy based on experience and ability, and subject to strict discipline from its central office, the English Excise more closely approximated to Max Weber's idea of bureaucracy than any other government agency in eighteenth-century Europe'.[17]

In short, George entered into a kingdom whose growing riches could be tapped by the state. It was also a kingdom that had just emerged victorious from more than a decade of warfare. The Whigs – and George with them – might whine about 'the unsuitable conclusion of a war ... attended with such unparalleled successes',[18] but the fact was that most war aims had been achieved, along with some unplanned bonuses. The danger of the Spanish and French thrones being united under one sovereign had been averted; the Protestant succession in Britain had been given international recognition; the

1. George I in his coronation robes, by Kneller

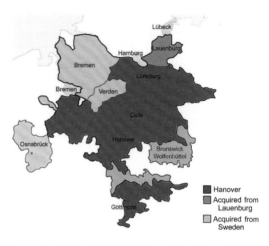

2. The electorate of Hanover

Lübeck
Hamburg
Lauenburg
Bremen
Lüneburg
Bremen
Verden
Celle
Osnabrück
Hanover
Brunswick Wolfenbüttel
Göttingen

Hanover
Acquired from Lauenburg
Acquired from Sweden

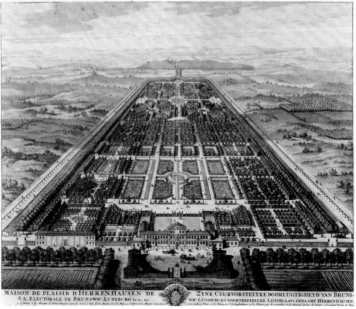

MAISON DE PLAISIR D HERRENHAUSEN DE S.A. ELECTORALE DE BRUNSWIC LUNEBURG ... ZYNE CEURVORSTELYKE DOORLUGTIGHEYD VAN BRUNS-WIC LUNENBURG VOORTREFFELYKE LUSTPLAATS GENAAMT HERRENHAUSEN.

3. Herrenhausen

4. George's father:
Elector Ernst August

5. George's mother:
Electress Sophia

6. George in 1680, aged twenty

7. George's wife Sophia Dorothea with their children, Georg August, the future George II, and Sophia Dorothea, the future Queen of Prussia

8. Hunting at Göhrde

9. George with his son Georg August, the future George II, and daughter-in-law Caroline

10. George and the line of succession

11. Kensington Palace

12. Britain as a great power: the Spanish fleet is destroyed at the Battle of Cape Passaro, Sicily, 11 August 1718

13. Greenwich, the Upper Hall: the glorification of George I and the house of Hanover by James Thornhill

Pretender had been banished from France; the former 'Spanish Netherlands' had been turned into an Austrian-ruled buffer against French expansion and further protected by Dutch-garrisoned fortresses; the conquest of Minorca and Gibraltar had secured naval domination of the western Mediterranean; recognition of British control of the Hudson Bay territory and the return of Nova Scotia and Newfoundland encouraged the belief that all North America could soon be wrested from the French; in the Caribbean the acquisition of the island of St Kitts pointed the way to further expansion; the transfer from France of the right to export African slaves to Spanish colonies (the *Asiento de negros*) symbolized the defeat of the threat that Spain would become a French satellite. Following naval victories at Vigo Bay in northern Spain in October 1702 and off Malaga in August 1704, Britannia ruled the waves.

With western and southern Europe now at peace, great-power attention switched to the north and east, where the 'Great Northern War' had been raging since 1700 and was showing no signs of abating. No one looked on with keener interest than the Elector of Hanover. Trying to provide a coherent narrative of a conflict whose theatre sprawled from Norway to the Black Sea has defeated generations of historians, yielding only some of the great unreadables of European historiography.[19] Using very broad brush-strokes, the war can be summarized as a struggle for the domination of the Baltic Sea between Sweden, whose empire in 1700 covered most of the territory around its eastern and southern shores, and a number of predators led by Peter the Great of Russia. What turned out to be the decisive moment came on 27 June 1709, when the latter inflicted a crushing defeat on Charles XII of Sweden at Poltava in Ukraine. When the news reached Hanover, Leibniz observed: 'you can imagine how the great revolution in the north has astounded people. It is being said that the Tsar will be formidable to the whole of Europe, that he will be a sort of Turk of the North.'[20] That status was delayed, for two years later Peter only narrowly escaped disaster at the hands of the Turks on the River Prut in Moldavia. Fortunately, George's role in this protracted conflict can be outlined concisely. It should be stressed at the outset that the policies pursued were very much his own. He arrived equipped not only with far more knowledge of the region than his English ministers but with the determination to make use of it. When Townshend tried to take an independent initiative, he was promptly demoted.[21]

His main aim was to gain from the wreckage of the Swedish Empire the duchies of Bremen and Verden, two secularized prince-bishoprics assigned to Sweden at the Peace of Westphalia in 1648. Situated between the Weser and Elbe rivers, whose mouths they commanded, immediately to the north of the main Hanoverian lands, they were extensive, fertile, prosperous and strategically important. In 1712, Frederick IV of Denmark had occupied Bremen and part of Verden, prompting Elector Georg Ludwig to send troops into what was left of the latter. To help him secure both duchies, he could draw on three important assets. Firstly, Hanover was much less vulnerable to Swedish retaliation than was Denmark. Following his defeat at

Poltava, Charles XII had taken refuge in the Ottoman Empire, leaving Sweden to manage as best it could without him. But in the very same month that George arrived in England – September 1714 – Charles set out on an amazing return journey, taking just fifteen days to cross Europe from Constantinople to Stralsund on the Baltic. This was bad news for George, but far worse news for Frederick IV.

Secondly, once released from the war against France by the Peace of Baden of September 1714, George could redirect the Hanoverian army of about 15,000 veterans to lend muscle to his diplomatic initiatives. Thirdly and most importantly, he could now draw on the incomparably greater resources of his new kingdom. Here he knew he had to be careful. The Act of Settlement of 1701 had expressly forbidden any use of English troops in the service of 'any dominions or territories which do not belong to the Crown of England, without the consent of Parliament'. Luckily for George, the interests of his two dominions intersected. Not for the first time, the mercurial Charles XII had come to the assistance of his enemies. Even before George had reached England, the Council of Regency had called on him to take action to correct 'the unfortunate condition of your subjects of Great Britain trading to the Balticke Sea, whose ships and effects are daily seized by the Swedish men of war and privateers'.[22] In 1714 alone, Swedish privateers had seized 107 British ships in the Baltic.[23] Just to show that this could not be explained away as freelance piracy, in February 1715 Charles helped by issuing an 'Ordinance of Privateers'. As the British resident at Stockholm pointed out, this meant that no merchant vessel could enter the Baltic without being made a prize.[24] George was both unscrupulous and skilful in exploiting this grey area. In May he took advantage of Frederick IV's fear of a Sweden rejuvenated by the return of Charles XII to extract an agreement that both Bremen and Verden would be ceded to Hanover in return for his electorate joining the war and a substantial cash payment.[25] Although no mention was made of naval assistance, Sir John Norris was sent to the Baltic with a powerful squadron of twenty warships, seven of them ships of the line.[26] In the official instructions he took with him, there was mention only of escorting a convoy and breaking the Swedish blockade of the eastern Baltic ports. It is very likely, however, that Norris was given orders from King George orally by Robethon or Bernstorff, or both, to take a much more forward line against the Swedes.[27]

Thus began several years of complex diplomacy and intermittent military activity. Their tortuous course was complicated by intense personal animosity. Each of the major players – George, his son-in-law Frederick William I, King of Prussia, Peter the Great and Charles XII – was a strong character with a depressing capacity for hatred. The violent antipathy the first three showed to their heirs was replicated in their relations with each other, Charles being exempted from this club of monstrous fathers only by his unwillingness or inability to procreate. The difficulty George experienced in persuading his son-in-law to honour agreements stemmed as much from mutual dislike as from a clash of interests. A massive stroke of luck for all concerned was the violent death of Charles XII on 30

November 1718. His unpredictability and sheer love of warfare meant that there could be no prospect of a durable peace so long as he was alive. Equally mercurial was the terrifying Tsar Peter, whose quixotic support for the despotic Duke of Mecklenburg, reinforced by a Russian army wintering in the duchy to the east of Hanover, caused George and the Hanoverians acute anxiety in 1716–17.

After years of inconsequential toing and froing, it all came together for George in the summer of 1719. With Sweden weakened by domestic political instability following the death of Charles, and threatened now with an imminent Russian invasion, Queen Ulrika Eleonora and her ministers were at last receptive to George's demands. In return for naval and diplomatic assistance and a substantial cash payment, on 29 August a treaty was signed ceding Bremen and Verden to Hanover. Decisive in closing the deal was the appearance off Stockholm of Sir John Norris and fifteen ships of the line to scare off the Russians.[28] It was facilitated by the artful diplomacy of Lord Carteret, whose arguments were reinforced by hefty bribes paid to Swedish senators.[29] There was more success for Carteret and his superior, Secretary of State Stanhope, in the summer of the following year, when they mediated peace between Denmark and Sweden. It was also their last, for they proved unable to make good their promise to the Swedes to force Peter the Great to disgorge at least some of the territory he had conquered. When the Great Northern War came to an end with the Peace of Nystad on 30 August 1721, Russian domination of the eastern Baltic was confirmed.[30]

Two questions remain. Firstly, could George have secured Bremen and Verden for Hanover if he had not been King of England? The answer to that must be an emphatic no. Without the formidable combination of British diplomacy and the Royal Navy, Sweden could not have been coerced, Prussia could not have been brought on side, and a Russian veto could not have been excluded. Secondly, were British interests sacrificed to Hanover? The answer here is less unequivocal. Given Swedish attacks on British commerce, it was clearly advantageous for Bremen and Verden to be transferred to Hanoverian ownership, at least in the short term. Charles XII had demonstrated his hostility to Britain in general and George in particular by his encouragement of privateering and support for the Jacobites. This Anglophobia may well have been structural as well as personal, for Sweden had long been a traditional ally of France, and was to remain so. It was less obvious that Russian hegemony in the Baltic was preferable to Swedish. That the importance of the Baltic as a source of naval stores increased rapidly with the expansion of the navy and merchant marine, and that British trade with the region boomed throughout the following century, does not prove very much, for this might have happened anyway.

More generally, it can be argued plausibly that Tory complaints that the Hanoverian lands acted as an incubus, sucking Britain into costly continental wars, were misplaced. Quite apart from the substantial human and material resources offered by the electorate in wartime, the need to safeguard its interests prevented that instinctive isolationism that is never glorious and often very dangerous. As

Brendan Simms has concluded, 'the Hanoverian connection not only enabled Britain to defeat the continental hegemons but was actually essential to the defence of her overseas empire'.[31] William Pitt the Elder was right to claim, following the victories of the Seven Years War, that 'had the armies of France not been employed in Germany, they would have been transported to America ... America had been conquered in Germany'.[32]

Away from the Baltic, Hanoverian interests were less influential. Perhaps surprisingly, the Great Northern War and the War of the Spanish Succession had run on parallel tracks that rarely threatened to converge. The latter had come to a messy end, leaving a messy peace that needed to be tidied up. The Habsburg Emperor Charles VI had refused to accept the separate peace made by Britain and the Dutch Republic, insisting on fighting a further fruitless year before succumbing to reality at the Peace of Rastatt in March 1714.[33] Symptomatic of its inconclusive nature was the refusal of Charles to recognize Philip V as King of Spain, referring to him instead as the 'Duke of Anjou', and the reciprocal insult offered by Philip when referring to Charles as 'Archduke'. After a generation of immensely destructive wars, it was in everyone's interest to promote formal peace into actual pacification. To the fore were King George and his British ministers, determined to establish long-term stability, if necessary by active intervention in continental affairs.

Their watchword was the 'balance of power', a protean but popular concept that had just appeared for the first time in an international treaty when the Peace of Utrecht proclaimed that its aim was 'to settle and establish the peace and tranquillity of Christendom by an equal balance of power (which is the best and most solid foundation of a mutual friendship, and of a concord which will be lasting on all sides)'.[34] It was underpinned by the belief that a change in one part of Europe affected the whole, and so the whole must be monitored by all. More specifically, it meant that any threat of that great bugbear 'universal monarchy' must be countered by a coalition of the threatened. In Trevelyan's succinct definition, it was 'the need to secure the safety of our small island by preventing the predominance of any one state on the Continent'.[35] As practised by William III, that meant organizing armed resistance to the overweening power of Louis XIV. It was an activist policy graphically advocated by the Whig polemicist John Toland: 'as for the Balance we must undoubtedly do our best to preserve it steddy, or if the rest of *Europe* falls into one Scale, we must soon be deprest by the irresistible Weight; and if we stand by, as unconcern'd Spectators, till this work is done, the greatest favor we must expect from our Neutrality, will be, like *Ulysses* in the Cave of *Polyphemus*, to be the last devour'd, which is but a miserable and unmanly Consolation'.[36] It was a belief shared by Tories, for example by Bolingbroke, who in 1727 lauded the balance of power as one of 'the original, everlasting principles of British politics'.[37]

Given this objective, George was lucky to come to the throne at a time when the War of the Spanish Succession had just denied hegemony to both Habsburgs and Bourbons. He could step forward as the 'rejoicing third' (*tertius gaudens*), holding the balance between the two. The mission he chose to accept was to reconcile the two former combatants by dealing with the unresolved issues and thus make the world, especially the Mediterranean, safe for British merchants. Unfortunately, he was confronted by two exceptionally intractable rulers. Charles VI had reigned in Spain for six years and could not accept the loss, symbolically imposing the gloomy Spanish etiquette on his new court in Vienna, to which he moved on the death of his brother Joseph in 1711. The priapic new King of Spain, Philip V, was in thrall to his lusty second wife Elizabeth Farnese of Parma, whom he married in 1714. Using sex to dominate her husband to a degree achieved by very few consorts, she exploited the resources of her new country to carve out a patrimony for the two sons she bore him – Don Carlos in 1716 and Don Philip in 1720. Neither seemed likely to succeed to the Spanish throne, as Philip already had two surviving sons by his first marriage, so she turned her attention to Italy.[38] On the credit side, George could draw on the support of the French regent, the Duke of Orléans, ever anxious to protect his chance of succeeding to the throne if the infant Louis XV should die.

A first success for British diplomacy was the 'Barrier Treaty' of November 1715, an agreement between Charles VI and the Dutch Republic to assign to the latter a number of fortresses in the Austrian Netherlands to serve as a bulwark against any future French invasion (when it came, in 1745, they proved to be useless). Extended negotiations with France followed, resulting in a treaty of November 1716, by which the French agreed to renounce any further support for the Jacobites, send the Pretender across the Alps to Rome and co-operate with the British in resolving international disputes. An early bonus for George was assistance in the Baltic for the assertion of Hanoverian interests against Russia.[39] The two new allies, intermittently supported by the Dutch, now turned their attention to banging Habsburg and Bourbon heads together. Charles VI proved the more amenable, not least because from early 1716 he was at war with the Turks. In August 1718, he joined the so-called 'Quadruple Alliance' with France and Britain to impose a settlement on the recalcitrant Spanish.[40] In the previous year, the latter had taken advantage of Austrian preoccupation with the Balkans to invade and occupy Sardinia. In 1718 they repeated the exercise in Sicily.

The arrival of Nemesis was not long delayed. Her first appearance came on 11 August 1718, when a British squadron commanded by Admiral Byng destroyed the Spanish fleet off Cape Passaro, capturing seven ships of the line in open waters and then destroying the remaining seven that sought refuge inshore. Two years of horror followed for Sicily, both for the marooned Spanish army and their involuntary hosts, until the inevitable surrender was signed. Meanwhile, in 1719 a British expeditionary force landed in Galicia, taking Vigo and Pontevedra, and a French army invaded the Basque country, taking San Sebastian. Very reluctantly, Philip V and his queen capitulated. The long-delayed adjustments to the Utrecht-Rastatt-Baden treaties now followed. Philip V renounced any claims to Italy or the southern Netherlands, but the succession to the duchies of Parma and Tuscany was assigned to Don Carlos; Charles VI finally abandoned his claim to the Spanish throne but received Sicily; Victor Amadeus II of Savoy had to give up the latter but received Sardinia in exchange and kept his royal title. Given the long-standing hostility between the two peace-makers, this imposition of a *pax franco-britannica* on Europe was nothing less than remarkable and showed what could be achieved when the 'natural and necessary enemies' (as Lord Stair described France and Britain in 1717) co-operated.[41]

By 1721 there was peace in the north and peace in the south, but implementing the small print of the agreements proved problematic. An international congress planned to assemble at Cambrai in 1722 did not actually start until 1724 and then got nowhere.[42] Part of the problem was the growing reluctance of Spain to trust the peace-makers and a corresponding willingness to try direct negotiations with Vienna. This process was accelerated in 1725 by an episode exemplifying the fairy-tale character of dynastic diplomacy. In 1721 the eleven-year-old Louis XV had been engaged to the four-year-old Spanish Infanta Mariana Victoria, daughter of Philip V and Elizabeth Farnese. This had been an initiative of Regent Orléans, who was eager to keep his royal charge from procreating for as long as possible. Following his death in 1723, King Louis's new chief minister, the Duke of Bourbon, was just as keen to see a royal heir produced as soon as possible, so the engagement was cancelled and the Infanta returned to Spain. Not unreasonably, the Spanish took violent exception to this insult. Charles VI responded to their advances promptly and a treaty of alliance was agreed at the end of April 1725.

This was very bad news for George. Not only did the Austro-Spanish rapprochement show that his days as arbiter of Europe were over, it also brought the Jacobite spectre back to life. Even more serious was the commercial threat posed by the 'Ostend Company', founded by the Austrians in 1722 as a rival to the British East India Company. Already showing signs of promise, the opening of Spanish markets in South America to its ships prompted a declaration by the House of Commons that it was aimed at 'the entire destruction of the British trade' and calls from the press to George to 'destroy this cockatrice whilst young'.[43] His response was the 'Hanover Alliance', formed in September 1725 by Britain, France, Hanover and Prussia and later joined by the Dutch Republic, Denmark and Sweden. To give it bite, 12,000 Hessian troops were hired for British service.[44] When Parliament assembled in January 1726, in his speech from the throne George presented the alliance as promoting both the national interest and the balance of power: 'by your Support and Assistance, I trust in God, I shall be able not only to secure to My own Subjects the Enjoyment of many valuable Rights and Privileges, long since acquired for them by the most solemn Treaties; but effectually to preserve the Peace and Balance of *Europe*, the only View and End of all My Endeavours'.[45]

Two disappointments in 1726 indicated an uphill struggle. In August, Charles VI secured an alliance with Russia, now ruled by Peter the Great's widow as Catherine I. In October, Frederick William I of Prussia defected from the

Hanover Alliance, lured by Austrian promises of support for his claims to the German duchies of Jülich and Berg. In the longer run, however, more important was the support George received from the French, concerned about the threat to their own East India Company. Together they imposed their will. With Austrian military preparations in chaos, denied support by the Holy Roman Empire and afraid that his Russian alliance was about to collapse following the death of the tsarina, Charles VI ran up the white flag. On 31 May 1727 he agreed to 'suspend' the Ostend Company for seven years and to cancel his commercial agreements with the Spanish. A desultory attempt by the latter to besiege Gibraltar was abandoned on 12 June.[46] George had died the previous day.

6
Conclusion

As a two-centre sovereign, it was fitting that George should have died in transit. Still apparently hale and hearty at the age of sixty-seven, he had reached Delden in the Dutch Republic on his way back to Hanover when he began to feel unwell. Insisting on proceeding, he was then felled by a stroke, from which he recovered consciousness only long enough to mutter his last words – 'It's all up with me' (*C'est fait de moi*). He died less than two days later, on 11 June, at Osnabrück. Taking the body back to London for a state funeral does not seem to have been considered. His heart had always been in Hanover figuratively, and that was where it was left physically, buried next to his mother in the family vault of the chapel of the Leine Palace.[1]

Also in 1727, Sir James Thornhill completed his great cycle of frescoes in the Painted Hall at Greenwich, on which he had been working for the past twenty years. With good reason this has been hailed as 'the most effective piece of Baroque decorative painting in England'.[2] There are three major frescoes – the ceiling of the Lower Hall depicting William and Mary, the ceiling of the Upper Hall depicting Queen Anne and her consort Prince George of

Denmark, and – as a visual climax – the west wall of the Upper Hall depicting George I and his family. Luckily, Thornhill spelled out in some detail exactly what he was representing in a pamphlet entitled *An explanation of the painting in the Royal-Hospital at Greenwich*. On the side wall of the Upper Hall, Thornhill wrote, he depicted the 'ACCESSION or *Landing of King* GEORGE at Greenwich; on his Right-hand is PEACE, on his Left-hand HAPPINESS; he is led on by TRUTH and JUSTICE, RELIGION, and LIBERTY; before him falls REBELLION'. The main fresco depicts Providence presenting George with the sceptre and the goddess Astrea 'alluding to JUSTICE and the *Golden Age* restored, who is on her Right-hand pouring forth *Riches*, etc. from a *Cornucopia*', while 'PEACE and PLENTY are offering at his *Majesty's* Feet: the little GENII of PAINTING, POETRY AND MUSICK, represented by the Three young princesses: round the *Cornucopia* are Prince *William* and his other Sisters playing with a Dove, shewing the Love and Harmony in this illustrious Family'.[3]

Eyebrows must have been raised at such praise for a family patently more dysfunctional than illustrious, but otherwise the images and comments chimed well with the self-image of English public opinion. For in this decorative scheme at Greenwich are to be found all the ingredients of British reason of state – true religion, liberty, property, prosperity, cultural distinction and naval power. There was enough reality supporting this baroque hyperbole to save it from ridicule. Indeed, the Painted Hall became a major tourist attraction. Even before the frescoes were complete, Richard Steele made the trip downstream with a party of friends to view 'that famous Ceiling' and recorded 'the whole raises in the Spectator the most lively Images of Glory and Victory, and cannot be beheld without much Passion and Emotion'.[4]

Although George's visual apotheosis was certainly more than he deserved, it did advertise how lucky he had been. Born to the youngest of four sons of a minor duke, one stroke of good fortune after another had taken him to be, first, one of the most prestigious princes in the Holy Roman Empire of the German Nation, and then the sovereign of three kingdoms and thus ruler of what was rapidly becoming the most prosperous and powerful empire in the world. Admittedly, most of the heavy lifting had been done before he reached London, and much of the subsequent achievement must be credited to the talented ministers he inherited. Yet he should not be dismissed as an accidental hero. Happily, gone are the days when he could be derided by J. H. Plumb as 'very stupid, and lacking interest in the arts, save music'.[5] Against that crude distortion can be set the judicious verdict of Jonathan Keates: 'remote and charmless as George may have seemed in public, he was also refined, astute and politically adept, earning loyalty and admiration from his English ministers and universal respect from the various ruling princes of Europe'.[6] From Hanover he brought with him a strong will, knowledge and experience of foreign and military affairs, and the kind of unexciting but solid virtues that played well with most of his English subjects. The eighteenth century was to end with most other thrones tottering or in ruins. Only the

Hanoverian dynasty had progressed to stand four-square on power, prosperity, religious pluralism and liberty. George I had played a crucial role in that process, mostly for what he was not, but in part for what he was: a king who knew how to ride his luck.

Notes

I. HANOVER

1. Karl Otmar Freiherr von Aretin, *Das Alte Reich 1648–1806*, vol. 2: *Kaisertradition und österreichische Großmachtpolitik (1684–1745)* (Stuttgart: Klett-Cotta, 1997), p. 60.
2. Georg Schnath, Rudolf Hillebrecht and Helmut Plath, *Das Leineschloss: Kloster, Fürstensitz, Landtagsgebäude* (Hanover: Hahnsche Buchhandlung, 1962), p. 61.
3. Rosenmarie Elisabeth Wallbrecht, *Das Theater des Barock-Zeitalters an den welfischen Höfen Hannover und Celle* (Hildesheim: Lax Verlag, 1974), pp. 46–54.
4. Barbara Arciszewska, *The Hanoverian Court and the Triumph of Palladio: The Palladian Revival, Hanover and England c.1700* (Warsaw: Wydawnictwo DiG, 2002), p. 40.
5. Eike Christian Hirsch, *Der berühmte Herr Leibniz: Eine Biographie* (Munich: C. H. Beck, 2007), p. 187.
6. Wallbrecht, *Das Theater des Barock-Zeitalters*, p. 14.
7. Marieanne von König (ed.), *Herrenhausen: Die königlichen Gärten in Hannover* (Göttingen: Wallstein Verlag, 2006), pp. 23–4.
8. Annette von Stieglitz, 'Höfisch-barocke Feste in Herrenhausen', in Hans-Dieter Schmid (ed.), *Feste und Feiern in Hannover* (Bielefeld: Verlag für Regionalgeschichte, 1995), p. 109.
9. Heiko Lass and Margret Scharrer, 'Selbstdarstellung und Repräsentation der Welfen', in Jochen Meiners (ed.), *Als die Royals aus Hannover kamen*, 4 vols (Dresden: Katja Lembke und Niedersächsisches Landesmuseum Hannover, 2014), vol. 1: *Reif für die Insel – Das Haus vom Herzogtum Braunschweig-Lüneburg auf dem Weg nach London*, p. 99.
10. Carl Möller, 'Sophie von der Pfalz, "Madame d'Osnabruc" und Garantin der Erhöhung des Welfenhauses', in Franz-Joachim Verspohl (ed.), *Das Osnabrücker Schloss: Stadtresidenz, Villa, Verwaltungssitz* (Osnabrück: Rasch, 1991), p. 119.
11. Hirsch, *Der berühmte Herr Leibniz*, p. 182.
12. Ragnhild Hatton, *George I: Elector and King* (London: Thames and Hudson, 1978), p. 29.
13. Andrew C. Thompson, *Britain, Hanover and the Protestant Interest 1688–1756* (Woodbridge: Boydell, 2006), p. 49.
14. Georg Schnath (ed.), *Briefwechsel der Kurfürstin Sophie von Hannover mit dem preussischen Königshause* (Berlin: K. J. Koehler, 1927), p. 11.

15. See the correspondence between Sophia and her brother, the Elector of the Palatinate, in Eduard Bodemann (ed.), *Briefwechsel der Herzogin Sophie von Hannover mit ihrem Bruder, dem Kurfürsten Karl Ludwig von der Pfalz und des letzteren mit seiner Schwägerin der Pfalzgräfin Anna* (Leipzig: S. Hirzel, 1885), pp. 361–2.

16. Eduard Bodemann (ed.), 'Briefe an den kurhannoverschen Minister Albr. Phil von dem Bussche von der Herzogin [Kurfürstin] Sophie, der Erbprinzessin Sophie Dorothee [Herzogin von Ahlden], der Aebtissin von Herford: Elisabeth von der Pfalz, Leibniz und der Frau von Harling, aus den Jahren 1677–1697', *Zeitschrift des Historischen Vereins für Niedersachsen* (1882), p. 148.

17. Hatton, *George I*, p. 49.

18. Georg Schnath, 'Der Fall Königsmarck. Leben, Ende und Nachlaß des Grafen Philipp Christoph Königsmarck im Licht neuer Funde', in *Ausgewählte Beiträge zur Landesgeschichte Niedersachsens* (Hildesheim: A. Lax, 1968), pp. 53–9.

19. Ibid., pp. 87–8. This is the most authoritative account of the affair. Schnath, archivist in Hanover, was able to show that the correspondence between Sophia Dorothea and Königsmarck discovered much later in a Swedish archive was genuine. Hatton, *George I*, p. 59, states that Montalban was given 150,000 talers, an improbably large sum, but this may be a misprint.

20. The most authoritative verdict is that of Graham Gibbs: 'Georg Ludwig seems to have played no part in the killing of Königsmarck on 1 July 1694', G. C. Gibbs, 'George I (1660–1727)', *Oxford Dictionary of National Biography* (Oxford: Oxford University Press, 2004); online edn May 2009 [http://www.oxforddnb.com/view/article/10538, accessed 26 October 2016].

21. Martin Wrede, 'The House of Brunswick-Lüneburg and the Holy Roman Empire: The making of a patriotic dynasty 1648–1714?', in Andreas Gestrich and Michael Schaich (eds), *The Hanoverian Succession: Dynastic Politics and Monarchical Culture* (Farnham: Ashgate, 2015), pp. 50–51.

22. Hirsch, *Der berühmte Herr Leibniz*, p. 172.

23. Michael-Andreas Tänzer, Arne Homann and Jens Mastnak, ' "Unsere brave Leute, so geblieben, werden nirgends gedacht, noch die lebendige gerümbt" – Krieg als Mittel welfischer Politik', in Meiners (ed.), *Als die Royals aus Hannover kamen*, vol. 1, p. 73.

24. Dietmar Storch, *Die Landstände des Fürstentums Calenberg-Göttingen 1680–1714* (Hildesheim: A. Lax, 1972), p. 111.

25. Gibbs, 'George I (1660–1727)'.

26. Luis von Sichart, *Geschichte der Königlich-Hannoverschen Armee*, vol. 2 (Hanover: Hahnsche Buchhandlung, 1870), pp. 293–6.

27. R. L. Arkell, *Caroline of Ansbach: George the Second's Queen* (Oxford: Oxford University Press, 1939), p. 42; Andrew Thompson, *George II: King and Elector* (New Haven and London: Yale University Press, 2011), p. 33.

28. Quoted in *Diary of Mary, Countess Cowper, Lady of the Bedchamber to the Princess of Wales* (London: John Murray, 1844), p. 24 n. 7.

29. von Aretin, *Das Alte Reich*, p. 150.

30. Sichart, *Geschichte der Königlich-Hannoverschen Armee*, vol. 2, pp. 248–73.

31. *Characters of the Court of Hannover with A Word or Two of SOME BODY else, which NO BODY has thought on* (London: J. Baker, 1714), p. 18.

2. THE HANOVERIAN SUCCESSION
IN ENGLAND

1. Quoted in Wallbrecht, *Das Theater des Barock-Zeitalters*, pp. 15–16.
2. E. Neville Williams, *The Eighteenth-Century Constitution 1688–1715: Documents and Commentary* (Cambridge: Cambridge University Press, 1960), p. 58.
3. Hatton, *George I*, pp. 75–7.
4. R. Pauli, 'Aktenstücke zur Thronbesteigung des Welfenhauses in England', *Zeitschrift des Historischen Vereins für Niedersachsen* (1883), pp. 69–74.
5. Joseph Hunter (ed.), *The diary of Ralph Thoresby, F.R.S, author of The Topography of Leeds (1677–1724)*, 2 vols (London: Colburn and Bentley, 1830), vol. 2, pp. 260–61.
6. F. Salomon, *Geschichte des letzten Ministeriums Königin Annas von England (1710–1714) und der englischen Thronfolgefrage* (Gotha: Friedrich Andreas Berthes, 1894), p. 66; Edward Gregg, *Queen Anne* (London: Ark Paperbacks, 1984), p. 363. Anne was the daughter of James II and his first wife, Anne Hyde; James the Pretender was the son of James II and his second wife, Mary of Modena.
7. H. T. Dickinson, *Bolingbroke* (London: Constable, 1970), pp. 117–18.
8. Eveline Cruickshanks and Howard Erskine-Hill, *The Atterbury Plot* (Basingstoke: Palgrave Macmillan, 2004), p. 6; Geoffrey Holmes, *The Trial of Doctor Sacheverell* (London: Eyre Methuen, 1973), p. 42.
9. Henry Hallam, *The Constitutional History of England* (London: Ward, Lock, Bowde, 1893), p. 739; G. M. Trevelyan, *England under Queen Anne*, vol. 1: *Blenheim* (London: Longmans Green, 1965), p. 185.
10. Graham C. Gibbs, 'Union Hanover/England. Accession to the throne and change of rulers: determining factors in the establishment and continuation of the personal union', in Rex Rexheuser (ed.), *Die Personalunionen von Sachsen-Polen 1697–1763 und Hannover-England 1714–1837: Ein Vergleich* (Wiesbaden: Harrassowitz, 2005), p. 249.
11. Hugh Trevor-Roper, *Archbishop Laud 1573–1645*, 3rd edn (London: Macmillan, 1988), p. 71.
12. Louis-Charles Fougeret de Montbron, *Préservatif contre l'anglomanie* ('À Minorque', 1757), p. 52.
13. Quoted in David Ogg, *England in the Reigns of James II and William III* (Oxford: Oxford University Press, 1969), p. 484.
14. James Gutheridge, *The Church of England's, or the Plain Man's Advice to the Jacobites with a True Account of His Imperial Majesty, King George's Pedigree, His High and Noble Qualifications, and of His Royal Highness George Prince of Wales. With some Remarks on the Church of Rome* (London, 1716), pp. 10–11.
15. James Drake, *The history of the last Parliament. Began at Westminster, the tenth day of February, in the twelfth year of the reign of King William, An. Dom. 1700*, 2nd edn (London, 1702), p. 29. On the similarity of transubstantiation and consubstantiation, see Francis Atterbury's incendiary pamphlet *English advice to the freeholders of England* (London, 1714), p. 20.
16. Gibbs, 'Union Hanover/England', p. 251.

17. Adrian Lashmore-Davies (ed.), *The Unpublished Letters of Henry St John, First Viscount Bolingbroke*, 5 vols (London: Taylor and Francis, 2013), vol. 1, p. xi.
18. Dickinson, *Bolingbroke*, p. 123.
19. Ibid., p. 131.
20. Gregg, *Queen Anne*, p. 393.
21. As Lord Stanhope observed, it was Bolingbroke's ambition to become 'the modern Alcibiades'. Voltaire claimed that the most famous prostitute in London had exclaimed, when she heard that Bolingbroke had been appointed Secretary of State: '7,000 guineas a year my sisters and all for us!' – Philip Henry Stanhope Earl Stanhope [Lord Mahon], *History of England from the Peace of Utrecht to the Peace of Aix-la-Chapelle*, 5th edn, vol. 1 (London: John Murray, 1858), p. 68.
22. William Coxe, *Memoirs of the life and administration of Sir Robert Walpole, Earl of Orford*, new edn, vol. 2 (London: Longman, 1816), p. 78.
23. Quoted in Julian Hoppit, *A Land of Liberty? England 1689–1727* (Oxford: Oxford University Press, 2000), p. 384.
24. Geoffrey Holmes, *British Politics in the Age of Anne*, rev. edn (London: A. & C. Black, 1987), p. 283.
25. Geoffrey Holmes and Daniel Szechi, *The Age of Oligarchy: Pre-industrial Britain 1722–1783* (London: Longman, 1993), p. 48; Gregg, *Queen Anne*, p. 334.
26. Gibbs, 'George I (1660–1727)'.
27. Storch, *Die Landstände des Fürstentums Calenberg-Göttingen*, pp. 16, 108–9, 115–16, 141–6.
28. Ragnhild Hatton believed that she could show that George had a much better grasp of English than had been previously assumed, but her evidence was challenged effectively in a review by W. A. Speck in *The English Historical Review*, 94, 373 (October 1979), pp. 866–8.
29. Gibbs, 'George I (1660–1727)'.
30. W. A. Speck, *Stability and Strife: England 1714–1760* (London: Edward Arnold, 1977), p. 171.
31. Quoted in Hannah Smith, 'The Hanoverian Succession and the Politicisation of the British Army', in Gestrich and Schaich (eds), *The Hanoverian Succession*, p. 222.
32. Basil Williams, *Stanhope: A Study in Eighteenth-Century War and Diplomacy* (Oxford: Oxford University Press, 1932), pp. 175–83.
33. Stanhope, *History of England*, vol. 1, p. 159.
34. Hoppit, *A Land of Liberty?*, p. 396.
35. Christopher Duffy, 'The Jacobite wars 1708–1746', in Edward M. Spiers, Jeremy Crang and Matthew Strickland (eds), *A Military History of Scotland* (Edinburgh: Edinburgh University Press, 2014), p. 353.
36. Daniel Szechi, *The Jacobites* (Manchester: Manchester University Press, 1994), p. 78.
37. Stanhope, *History of England*, vol. 1, p. 183.
38. Edward Gregg, 'James Francis Edward (1688–1766)', *Oxford Dictionary of National Biography*; online edn May 2012 [http://www.oxforddnb.com/view/article/14594, accessed 3 October 2016].
39. 'Never was the wisdom of this ministry more clearly demonstrated than in the way in which it handled the Jacobite rebellion', J. H. Plumb, *Sir Robert Walpole*, vol. 1: *The Making of a Statesman* (London: Cresset, 1956), p. 217.
40. J. H. Shennan, *Philippe, Duke of Orléans, Regent of France 1715–23* (London: Thames and Hudson, 1979), p. 54.
41. H. T. Dickinson, 'The Jacobite challenge', in Michael Lynch (ed.), *Jacobitism and the '45* (London: Historical Association, 1995), p. 8.

42. Quoted in Speck, *Stability and Strife*, p. 152. As Speck concludes, 'For all the talk of popular Jacobitism, there is precious little evidence for it' (p. 166).

43. Williams, *Stanhope*, pp. 325–7.

44. T. M. Devine, *The Scottish Nation 1700–2000* (London: Allen Lane, 1999), pp. xx–xxi.

45. Howard Nenner, *The Right to be King: The Succession to the Crown of England 1603–1714* (Basingstoke: Macmillan, 1995), p. 240.

46. T. C. Smout, 'The road to union', in Geoffrey Holmes (ed.), *Britain after the Glorious Revolution* (London: Macmillan, 1969), p. 192.

47. Gabriel Glickman, 'Jacobitism and the Hanoverian monarchy', in Gestrich and Schaich (eds), *The Hanoverian Succession*, p. 241.

48. Stanhope, *History of England*, vol. 1, p. 62.

49. Devine, *The Scottish Nation*, p. 29.

50. Hatton, *George I*, p. 116, 179 n.

51. Thomas Bartlett, *Ireland: A History* (Cambridge: Cambridge University Press, 2010), p. 153.

52. Hatton, *George I*, p. 154.

53. T. W. Moody and W. E. Vaughan (eds), *A New History of Ireland*, vol. 4: *Eighteenth-Century Ireland 1691–1800* (Oxford: Oxford University Press, 1986), p. 111.

54. Hatton, *George I*, p. 290 n.

55. Quoted in Speck, *Stability and Strife*, p. 174.

56. Lucy Worsley, *Courtiers: The Secret History of Kensington Palace* (London: Faber, 2010), pp. 30, 83, 125, 130; Hatton, *George I*, p. 132.

57. Strangely, this old *canard* was repeated by J. H. Plumb – *Sir Robert Walpole*, vol. 1, p. 198 – which suggests that, not only did he know nothing of the German literature on George I, but he had not read all of the English-language material either. For an accurate biography see Matthew Kilburn, 'Kielmansegg, Sophia Charlotte von, *suo jure* countess of Darlington and *suo jure* countess of Leinster (1675–1725)', *Oxford Dictionary of National Biography*; online edn January 2008 [http://www.oxforddnb.com/view/article/76310, accessed 4 October 2016].

58. Hatton, *George I*, pp. 148, 155.

59. Trevelyan, *England under Queen Anne*, vol. 1, p. 80.

60. Gibbs, 'Union Hanover/England', p. 272.

61. Thompson, *Britain, Hanover and the Protestant Interest*, pp. 96–8.

62. Jeremy Black, 'The Catholic Threat and the British Press in the 1720s and 1730s', *Journal of Religious History*, 12 (1983), p. 371.

3. COURT, COUNTRY AND FAMILY MATTERS

1. Quoted in John M. Beattie, *The English Court in the Reign of George I* (Cambridge: Cambridge University Press, 1967), p. 9.

2. Hannah Smith, *Georgian Monarchy: Politics and Culture 1714–1760* (Cambridge: Cambridge University Press, 2006), p. 70.

3. Ibid., p. 68; H. M. Colvin and John Newman, 'The royal palaces, 1660–1782', in H. M. Colvin, J. Mordaunt Crook, Kerry Downes and John Newman, *The History of the King's Works*, vol. 5 (London: HMSO, 1976), p. 195.

4. Worsley, *Courtiers*, pp. 57, 77, 80–100.

5. David McKitterick, *Cambridge University Library: A History*, vol. 2 (Cambridge: Cambridge University Press, 1986), pp. 17, 151.

6. Victor Morgan, *A History of the University of Cambridge*, vol. 2: *1546–1750* (Cambridge: Cambridge University Press, 2004), p. 249; L. S. Sutherland, 'The Curriculum', in L. G. Mitchell and L. S. Sutherland (eds), *The History of the University of Oxford*, vol. 5: *The Eighteenth Century* (Oxford: Clarendon Press, 1986), p. 474.

7. See the brilliant analysis in John Adamson, 'The making of the Ancien Régime court 1500–1700', in John Adamson (ed.), *The Princely Courts of Europe: Ritual, Politics and Culture under the Ancien Régime 1500–1750* (London: Seven Dials, 2000), pp. 7–41.

8. Claudia Gold, *The King's Mistress: The True and Scandalous Story of the Woman who Stole the Heart of George I* (London: Quercus, 2012), pp. 119–20.

9. Beattie, *The English Court in the Reign of George I*, pp. 11–17.

10. Thompson, *George II*, p. 45.

11. J. M. Beattie, 'The Court of George I and English Politics, 1717–1720', *English Historical Review*, 81, 318 (January 1966), p. 26.

12. Schnath, Hillebrecht and Plath, *Das Leineschloss*, p. 79.

13. Donald Burrows and Robert D. Hume, 'George I, the Haymarket Opera Company and Handel's "Water Music" ', *Early Music*, 19, 3 (1991), pp. 326–7, 334.

14. Burrows has conjectured that the occasion was also intended to demonstrate that Handel's move from Hanoverian employment to London in 1710 had not been resented by George – *Handel* (Oxford: Oxford University Press, 1994), pp. 76–7.

15. Schnath, *Briefwechsel der Kurfürstin Sophie von Hannover mit dem preußischen Königshause*, p. 273.

16. Volkmar Koehler, 'Jagdschloß Göhrde', in *Niederdeutsche Beiträge zur Kunstgeschichte*, 8 (1969), p. 171.

17. Jürgen Delfs, 'Jagdarten' , in Norbert Steinau (ed.), *Jagd in der Lüneburger Heide: Beiträge zur Jagdgeschichte* (Celle: Bomann-Museum Celle und Suderburg-Hösseringen Landwirtschaftsmuseum Lüneburger Heide, 2007), p. 34.

18. Wallbrecht, *Das Theater des Barock-Zeitalters*, p. 102.

19. Gibbs, 'George I (1660–1727)'.

20. J. P. Hore, *The History of the Royal Buckhounds* (London: Remington & Co., 1893), p. 264.

21. Gibbs, 'George I (1660–1727)'.

22. Aubrey Newman, 'Two countries, one monarch: The union England/Hanover as the ruler's personal problem', in Rexheuser (ed.), *Die Personalunionen von Sachsen-Polen 1697–1763*, p. 361.

23. Stanhope, *History of England*, vol. 1, p. 245; Thompson, *George II*, pp. 47–8.

24. Hallam, *The Constitutional History of England*, p. 775. He was referring to Frederick, Prince of Wales, George I's grandson, but it applies just as well to his son.

25. Henry L. Snyder, 'Spencer, Charles, third earl of Sunderland (1675–1722)', *Oxford Dictionary of National Biography*; online edn May 2006 [http://www.oxforddnb.com/view/article/26117, accessed 6 October 2016].

26. Beattie, 'The Court of George I and English Politics', pp. 29, 33.

27. Hatton, *George I*, p. 204.
28. Beattie, 'The Court of George I and English Politics', p. 34.
29. The best accounts of this unedifying episode are to be found in Plumb, *Sir Robert Walpole*, vol. 1, pp. 259–60, and Thompson, *George II*, pp. 51–3.
30. Joanna Marschner, *Queen Caroline: Cultural Politics at the Early Eighteenth-Century Court* (New Haven and London: Yale University Press, 2014), p. 15.
31. Plumb, *Sir Robert Walpole*, vol. 1, p. 260.
32. Beattie, 'The Court of George I and English Politics', p. 36.
33. Quoted in Edward Impey, *Kensington Palace*, rev. edn (London and New York: Merrell, 2012), pp. 72–3.

4. WHIGS AND TORIES

1. The belief of some historians that the Tory Party was indeed a Jacobite party has been demolished comprehensively, by, for example, W. A. Speck in 'Whigs and Tories dim their glories: English political parties under the first two Georges', in John Cannon (ed.), *The Whig Ascendancy: Colloquies on Hanoverian England* (London: Edward Arnold, 1981), and Andrew Hanham, '"So few facts": Jacobites, Tories and the Pretender', *Parliamentary History*, 19, 2 (2000) pp. 233–57.
2. Estimates vary considerably. Speck, *Stability and Strife*, p. 177, gives the Tory majority as 65; Hoppit, *A Land of Liberty?*, p. 391, gives almost double that figure – 124.
3. Quoted in Dickinson, *Bolingbroke*, p. 144.
4. Atterbury, *English advice to the freeholders of England*, p. 19.
5. Jeremy Black, *Politics and Foreign Policy in the Age of George I, 1714–1727* (Farnham: Ashgate, 2014), p. 12.
6. William Edward Hartpole Lecky, *A History of England in the Eighteenth Century* (London: Longmans Green, 1892), vol. 1, p. 259.
7. Holmes, *The Trial of Doctor Sacheverell*, p. 275.
8. There is an exceedingly, perhaps excessively, sympathetic account of this farcical episode in Eveline Cruickshanks and Howard Erskine-Hill, *The Atterbury Plot* (London: Palgrave Macmillan, 2004), most of which was written by the former. Some idea of Dr Cruickshanks's attitude to the Jacobites can be gained from her observation that, when interrogated, the conspirators 'were much in the same position as members of the Resistance in Europe in the years 1940–44 who were questioned by the Germans', p. 198.
9. G. V. Bennett, 'Jacobitism and the rise of Walpole', in Neil McKendrick (ed.), *Historical Perspectives: Studies in English Thought and Society in Honour of J. H. Plumb* (London: Europa, 1974), p. 91.
10. Holmes, *The Trial of Doctor Sacheverell*, p. 267.
11. Williams, *Stanhope*, p. 393.
12. Ibid., pp. 225–6.
13. Lothar Kettenacker, 'Georg I.', in Peter Wende (ed.), *Englische Könige und Königinnen der Neuzeit: Von Heinrich VIII. bis Elisabeth II* (Munich: C. H. Beck, 2008), p. 196.
14. Quoted in Williams, *Stanhope*, p. 442.

15. Fritz Genzel, 'Studien zur Geschichte des Nordischen Krieges 1714–20, unter besonderer Berücksichtigung der Personalunion zwischen Grossbritannien und Hannover' (unpublished PhD dissertation, Bonn, 1951), p. 26.

16. Matthew Kilburn, 'Robethon, John (d. 1722)', Oxford Dictionary of National Biography; online edn May 2009 [http://www.oxforddnb.com/view/article/23821, accessed 10 October 2016].

17. J. F. Chance, 'John de Robethon and the Robethon Papers', English Historical Review, 13, 49 (1898), pp. 58–60.

18. In the judgement of Adolphus Ward, 'more than any other individual, Bothmer was responsible for the Hanoverian Succession' – A. W. Ward, 'Great Britain under George I', in A. W. Ward, G. W. Prothero and Stanley Leathes (eds), The Cambridge Modern History, vol. 6: The Eighteenth Century (Cambridge: Cambridge University Press, 1909), p. 12.

19. Andrew C. Thompson, 'Bothmer, Hans Kaspar von, Count Bothmer in the nobility of the Holy Roman empire (1656–1732)', Oxford Dictionary of National Biography; online edn January 2008 [http://www.oxforddnb.com/view/article/89690, accessed 10 October 2016].

20. Genzel, Studien zur Geschichte des Nordischen Krieges, p. 20.

21. Williams, Stanhope, p. 366.

22. Chance, 'John de Robethon', p. 61. See also Stanhope's remarks to the Duke of Newcastle quoted in Jeremy Black, The Hanoverians: The History of a Dynasty (London: Hambledon and London, 2004), p. 71.

23. R. J. Minney, 10 Downing Street: A House in History (London: Cassell, 1963), p. 33.

24. Williams, Stanhope, p. 416.

25. Stephen Taylor, 'Walpole, Robert, first earl of Orford (1676–1745)', Oxford Dictionary of National Biography; online edn January 2008 [http://www.oxforddnb.com/view/article/28601, accessed 10 October 2016].

26. Diary of Mary Countess Cowper, pp. 128–45. Plumb, Sir Robert Walpole, vol. 1, pp. 285–92 supplies a convenient summary, including many quotations from Lady Cowper's diary.

27. Diary of Mary Countess Cowper, p. 134.

28. Ibid., pp. 142–3.

29. Ibid., p. 145.

30. Impey, Kensington Palace, p. 73.

31. Plumb, Sir Robert Walpole, vol. 2, p. 65, n. 1.

32. P. G. M. Dickson, The Financial Revolution in England: A Study in the Development of Public Credit 1688–1756 (London: Macmillan, 1967), p. 197.

33. Ibid., p. 94.

34. Peter Dickson, 'The South Sea Bubble', History Today, May 1954, p. 328.

35. Black, The Hanoverians, p. 76.

36. Plumb, Sir Robert Walpole, vol. 1, p. 355 n. 1.

37. W. A. Speck and Matthew Kilburn, 'Promoters of the South Sea Bubble (act. 1720)', Oxford Dictionary of National Biography [http://www.oxforddnb.com/view/theme/92793, accessed 11 October 2016].

38. Unusually for a biographer, Plumb was at pains to play down Walpole's achievement and to ascribe his success to luck – Walpole, vol. 1, chs 8–9. Dickson, however, showed convincingly that Walpole really did deserve most of the credit – The Financial Revolution in England, chs 7–8. His general conclusion is on p. 176: 'There can be little doubt that Walpole was the main architect of these proposals, which

applied the harsh cautery of common sense to the soaring dreams and megalo-maniac expectations of the South Sea year.'

39. Linda Frey and Marsha Frey, 'Townshend, Charles, second Viscount Townshend (1674–1738)', *Oxford Dictionary of National Biography* [http://www.oxforddnb.com/view/article/27617, accessed 12 October 2016].

40. John Cannon, 'Carteret, John, second Earl Granville (1690–1763)', *Oxford Dictionary of National Biography;* online edn May 2006 [http://www.oxforddnb.com/view/article/4804, accessed 12 October 2016].

41. Dickson, *The Financial Revolution in England*, pp. 200–201.

42. Hoppit, *A Land of Liberty?*, p. 322.

5. THE SINEWS OF POWER AND FOREIGN POLICY

1. Trevelyan, *England under Queen Anne*, vol. 1, p. 24.

2. Ogg, *England in the Reigns of James II and William III*, p. 281.

3. Martin Daunton, 'The wealth of the nation', in Paul Langford (ed.), *The Short Oxford History of the British Isles: The Eighteenth Century* (Oxford: Oxford University Press, 2002), p. 158.

4. David Landes, *The Unbound Prometheus: Technological Change and Industrial Development in Western Europe from 1750 to the Present* (Cambridge: Cambridge University Press, 1969), p. 46.

5. Geoffrey Holmes, 'The achievement of stability: the social context of politics from the 1680s to the age of Walpole', in Cannon (ed.), *The Whig Ascendancy*, p. 6.

6. Hoppit, *A Land of Liberty?*, pp. 67, 266–7, 344, 353.

7. Dickson, *The Financial Revolution in England*, p. 13.

8. Geoffrey Holmes, 'Post-Revolution Britain and the Historian', in Holmes (ed.), *Britain after the Glorious Revolution*, p. 22.

9. Dickson, *The Financial Revolution in England*, p. 55.

10. Stanhope, *History of England*, vol. 1, p. 25.

11. Guy Rowlands, 'The economics of war: tax, trade and credit in pursuit of an acceptable peace', in Renger de Bruin and Maarten Brinkmann (eds), *Peace Was Made Here: The Treaties of Utrecht, Rastatt and Baden* (Petersberg: Michael Imhof Verlag, 2013), p. 36.

12. David Hayton, 'Contested kingdoms, 1699–1756', in Langford (ed.), *The Short Oxford History of the British Isles*, p. 42.

13. Richard Price, *British Society 1680–1880: Dynamism, Containment and Change* (Cambridge: Cambridge University Press, 1999), p. 142.

14. Martin Daunton, *Trusting Leviathan: The Politics of Taxation in Britain, 1799–1914* (Cambridge: Cambridge University Press, 2001), p. 1. Daunton was writing mainly about the nineteenth century, but his remarks apply *a fortiori* to the earlier period.

15. J. G. A. Pocock, 'The varieties of Whiggism from Exclusion to Reform: a history of ideology and discourse', in J. G. A. Pocock, *Virtue, Commerce, and History:*

Essays on Political Thought and History, Chiefly in the Eighteenth Century (Cambridge: Cambridge University Press, 1985), p. 222.

16. Hoppit, *A Land of Liberty?*, pp. 125, 264.

17. John Brewer, *The Sinews of Power: War, Money and the English State 1688–1783* (London: Unwin Hyman, 1989), p. 68.

18. The phrase comes from the Address of Thanks presented to George following the opening of Parliament on 17 March 1715. The address was composed by a committee chaired by Walpole, 'First Parliament of George I: First session (part 1 of 3) – begins 17/3/1715', in *The History and Proceedings of the House of Commons*, vol. 6, *1714–1727* (London: Chandler, 1742), pp. 9–47. *British History Online* http://www.british-history.ac.uk/commons-hist-proceedings/vol6/p9-47 [accessed 17 October 2016].

19. The most lucid account of the northern question is to be found in Janet Hartley, *Charles Whitworth: Diplomat in the Age of Peter the Great* (Aldershot: Ashgate, 2002).

20. Quoted in Lindsey Hughes, *Russia in the Age of Peter the Great* (New Haven and London: Yale University Press, 1998), p. 40.

21. See the review of Hatton, *George I*, by W. A. Speck in *The English Historical Review*, 94, 373 (October 1979), pp. 866–8.

22. Quoted in Williams, *Stanhope*, p. 159.

23. Hartley, *Charles Whitworth*, p. 119.

24. J. F. Chance, 'The foreign policy of George I', in Ward, Prothero and Leathes (eds), *The Cambridge Modern History*, vol. 6, p. 24.

25. Genzel, *Studien zur Geschichte des Nordischen Krieges*, p. 603.

26. David Denis Aldridge, *Admiral Sir John Norris and the British Naval Expeditions to the Baltic Sea 1715–1727*, ed. Leos Müller and Patrick Salmon (Lund: Nordic Academic Press, 2009), p. 64.

27. Williams, *Stanhope*, p. 232; Chance, 'The foreign policy of George I', p. 24.

28. Genzel, *Studien zur Geschichte des Nordischen Krieges*, pp. 143–54.

29. Chance, 'The foreign policy of George I', p. 36.

30. Williams, *Stanhope*, p. 428.

31. Brendan Simms, 'Hanover in British policy 1714–1783: Interests and aims of the protagonists', in Rexheuser (ed.), *Die Personalunionen von Sachsen-Polen 1697–1763*, p. 134.

32. Quoted in Brendan Simms and Torsten Riotte (eds), *The Hanoverian Dimension in British History, 1714–1837* (Cambridge: Cambridge University Press, 2007), p. 55. For an alternative maritime perspective, see N. A. M. Rodger, 'The continental commitment in the eighteenth century', in L. Freedman, P. Hayes and R. O'Neill (eds), *War, Strategy and International Relations: Essays in Honour of Sir Michael Howard* (Oxford: Clarendon Press, 1992), p. 53.

33. Peace between France and the Habsburg monarchy was signed at Rastatt on 7 March 1714 and between France and the Holy Roman Empire at Baden on 7 September 1714.

34. Heinz Duchhardt, 'England-Hannover und der europäische Friede 1714–1748', in Adolf Birke and Kurt Kluxen (eds), *England und Hannover/ England and Hanover* (Munich, London, New York and Oxford: De Gruyter, 1986), p. 128. It was also the first international treaty to be drafted in the French language. It can be found in English translation at https://en.wikisource.org/wiki/Peace_and_Friendship_Treaty_of_Utrecht_between_Spain_and_Great_Britain.

35. Trevelyan, *England under Queen Anne*, vol. 1, p. 118.

36. Toland, John, *The art of governing by partys: particularly, in religion, in politics, in Parlament, on the Bench, and in the Ministry; with the ill effects of partys on the people in general, the King in particular, and all our foren Affairs; as well as on our Credit and Trade, in Peace or War* (London: Bernard Lintott, 1701), p. 143.

37. Quoted in G. C. Gibbs, 'The Revolution in foreign policy', in Holmes (ed.), *Britain after the Glorious Revolution*, p. 62.

38. For a more sympathetic treatment of Philip V, see Christopher Storrs, *The Spanish Resurgence 1713–1748* (New Haven and London: Yale University Press, 2016).

39. Williams, *Stanhope*, pp. 227–9. Despite over-emphasis on Stanhope's role, this is the best account of British diplomacy during this period.

40. G. C. Gibbs, 'Parliament and the Treaty of Quadruple Alliance', in Ragnhild Hatton and J. S. Bromley (eds), *William III and Louis XIV: Essays by and for Mark A. Thomson* (Liverpool: Liverpool University Press, 1968), p. 287.

41. Duchhardt, 'England – Hannover und der europäische Friede 1714–1748', p. 134.

42. The best account of the extremely confusing and inconsequential diplomacy of these years is to be found in Derek McKay and H. M. Scott, *The Rise of the Great Powers 1648–1815* (London: Longman, 1983), pp. 118–34.

43. Gerald B. Hertz, 'England and the Ostend Company', *English Historical Review*, 22, 86 (1907), pp. 265–6.

44. Speck, *Stability and Strife*, p. 232.

45. http://www.british-history.ac.uk/lords-jrnl/vol22/pp574-583.

46. McKay and Scott, *The Rise of the Great Powers*, p. 133.

6. CONCLUSION

1. Gibbs, 'George I (1660–1727)'.

2. John Bold, *Greenwich: An Architectural History of the Royal Hospital for Seamen and the Queen's House* (New Haven and London: Yale University Press, 2000), p. 1.

3. James Thornhill, *An explanation of the painting in the Royal-Hospital at Greenwich* (London, c.1730), p. 18.

4. Richard Steele, *The Lover*, in Walter Lewin (ed.), *The Lover, and Other Papers of Steele and Addison* (London: Walter Scott, 1887), pp. 155–9.

5. J. H. Plumb, *The First Four Georges* (London: Batsford, 1956), p. 60.

6. Jonathan Keates, *Handel, the Man and his Music* (London: Pimlico, 2009), p. 51.

Further Reading

Only titles written in English have been included. For German readers, a good place to start is the collection edited by Jochen Meiners: *Als die Royals aus Hannover kamen*, 4 vols (Dresden: Sandstein, 2014).

The standard biography of George I remains Ragnhild Hatton, *George I: Elector and King* (London: Thames and Hudson, 1978), based on extensive archival research and deep knowledge of the period. There is an excellent concise and penetrating biography by G. C. Gibbs in the *Oxford Dictionary of National Biography* (Oxford: Oxford University Press, 2004), which can be accessed online. There is also a good deal to be learned about both George and Hanover in Andrew Thompson's distinguished biography *George II: King and Elector* (New Haven and London: Yale University Press, 2011).

There are several first-rate general histories of Britain in the period, the best being W. A. Speck, *Stability and Strife: England 1714–1760* (London: Edward Arnold, 1977) and Julian Hoppit, *A Land of Liberty? England 1689–1727* (Oxford: Oxford University Press, 2000). Helpful collections of articles are Geoffrey Holmes (ed.), *Britain after the Glorious Revolution* (London: Macmillan, 1969); John Cannon (ed.), *The Whig Ascendancy: Colloquies on Hanoverian England* (London: Edward Arnold, 1981); Brendan Simms and Torsten Riotte (eds), *The Hanoverian Dimension in British History, 1714–1837* (Cambridge: Cambridge University Press, 2007); and Andreas Gestrich and Michael Schaich (eds),

The Hanoverian Succession: Dynastic Politics and Monarchical Culture (Farnham: Ashgate, 2015). Many of the contributions to Rex Rexheuser (ed.), *Die Personalunionen von Sachsen-Polen 1697–1763 und Hannover-England 1714–1837: Ein Vergleich* (Wiesbaden: Harrassowitz, 2005) are in English.

On the Hanoverian succession, indispensable are Edward Gregg's excellent biography of *Queen Anne* (London: Ark Paperbacks, 1984) and Howard Nenner's *The Right to be King: The Succession to the Crown of England 1603–1714* (Basingstoke: Macmillan, 1995).

Still essential for the court is John M. Beattie, *The English Court in the Reign of George I* (Cambridge: Cambridge University Press, 1967), and see also his article 'The Court of George I and English Politics, 1717–1720', *English Historical Review*, 81, 318 (January 1966). These can be supplemented by Barbara Arciszewska, *The Hanoverian Court and the Triumph of Palladio: The Palladian Revival, Hanover and England c.1700* (Warsaw: Wydawnictwo DiG, 2002); Lucy Worsley, *Courtiers: The Secret History of Kensington Palace* (London: Faber, 2010); Claudia Gold, *The King's Mistress: The True and Scandalous Story of the Woman who Stole the Heart of George I* (London: Quercus, 2012); and Joanna Marschner, *Queen Caroline: Cultural Politics at the Early Eighteenth-Century Court* (New Haven and London: Yale University Press, 2014). Especially illuminating is Hannah Smith, *Georgian Monarchy: Politics and Culture 1714–1760* (Cambridge: Cambridge University Press, 2006). On the buildings, see H. M. Colvin, J. Mordaunt Crook, Kerry Downes and John Newman, *The History of the King's Works*, vol. 5 (London: HMSO, 1976), and Edward Impey, *Kensington Palace*, revised edition (London and New York: Merrell, 2012).

On the financial revolution which made both George's inheritance so favourable and his foreign policy possible, see Peter Dickson's trailblazing *The Financial Revolution in England: A Study in the Development of Public Credit 1688–1756* (London: Macmillan,

1967), a work of great distinction. This can be supplemented by John Brewer, *The Sinews of Power: War, Money and the English State 1688–1783* (London: Unwin Hyman, 1989), and Martin Daunton, 'The wealth of the nation', in Paul Langford (ed.), *The Short Oxford History of the British Isles: The Eighteenth Century* (Oxford: Oxford University Press, 2002).

On domestic politics, still helpful is A. W. Ward, 'Great Britain under George I', in A. W. Ward, G. W. Prothero and Stanley Leathes (eds), *The Cambridge Modern History*, vol. 6: *The Eighteenth Century* (Cambridge: Cambridge University Press, 1909), and still indispensable is J. H. Plumb, *Sir Robert Walpole*, vol. 1: *The Making of a Statesman* and vol. 2: *The King's Minister* (London: Cresset, 1956 and 1960). There are numerous good articles in the *Oxford Dictionary of National Biography*; see especially Edward Gregg on the Pretender, Henry L. Snyder on Sunderland, A. A. Hanham on Stanhope, Matthew Kilburn on Robethon, Andrew C. Thompson on Bothmer, Stephen Taylor on Walpole, W. A. Speck and Matthew Kilburn on the promoters of the South Sea Bubble, Linda Frey and Marsha Frey on Townshend, and John Cannon on Carteret. On the Tories there is much to be found in H. T. Dickinson, *Bolingbroke* (London: Constable, 1970). On Jacobitism, a topic which still attracts polemical writing which tends to generate more heat than light, there are judicious assessments by Dickinson in his article 'The Jacobite challenge', in Michael Lynch (ed.), *Jacobitism and the '45* (London: Historical Association, 1995); Christopher Duffy, 'The Jacobite wars 1708–1746', in Edward M. Spiers, Jeremy Crang and Matthew Strickland (eds), *A Military History of Scotland* (Edinburgh: Edinburgh University Press, 2014); and Gabriel Glickman, 'Jacobitism and the Hanoverian monarchy' in the collection edited by Gestrich and Schaich listed above. On ecclesiastical politics, very helpful and much more general than the title suggests is Geoffrey Holmes, *The Trial of Doctor Sacheverell* (London: Eyre Methuen, 1973). Also illuminating is G. V. Bennett, 'Jacobitism and the rise of

Walpole', in Neil McKendrick, *Historical Perspectives: Studies in English Thought and Society in Honour of J. H. Plumb* (London: Europa, 1974). Two influential monographs by Linda Colley are *In Defiance of Oligarchy: The Tory Party 1714–60* (Cambridge: Cambridge University Press, 1982) and *Britons: Forging the Nation 1707–1837* (New Haven and London: Yale University Press, 1992).

On foreign policy the best general history is Derek McKay and H. M. Scott, *The Rise of the Great Powers 1648–1815* (London: Longman, 1983), which is both lucid and scholarly. Fundamental is G. C. Gibbs, 'The Revolution in foreign policy', in the collection *Britain after the Glorious Revolution* edited by Holmes and listed above. The contribution by J. F. Chance, 'The foreign policy of George I', to Ward, Prothero and Leathes (eds), *The Cambridge Modern History*, vol. 6 is immensely detailed, but so densely textured and turgid as to be almost unreadable. Two substantial and distinguished biographies which also reveal a great deal about the international relations of the period are Basil Williams, *Stanhope: A Study in Eighteenth-Century War and Diplomacy* (Oxford: Oxford University Press, 1932) and Janet Hartley, *Charles Whitworth: Diplomat in the Age of Peter the Great* (Aldershot: Ashgate, 2002). Two important monographs are Andrew C. Thompson, *Britain, Hanover and the Protestant Interest 1688–1756* (Woodbridge: Boydell, 2006) and David Denis Aldridge, *Admiral Sir John Norris and the British Naval Expeditions to the Baltic Sea 1715–1727*, edited by Leos Müller and Patrick Salmon (Lund: Nordic Academic Press, 2009). Very helpful is Robert Frost, *The Northern Wars: War, State and Society in Northeastern Europe, 1558–1721* (Harlow: Longman, 2000).

There is a formidable amount of writing on Scotland and Ireland in the period. Good introductions are David Hayton, 'Contested kingdoms, 1699–1756', in Langford (ed.), *The Short Oxford History of the British Isles*; T. M. Devine, *The Scottish Nation 1700–2000* (London: Allen Lane, 1999); T. W. Moody and W. E. Vaughan (eds),

A New History of Ireland, vol. 4: *Eighteenth-Century Ireland 1691–1800* (Oxford: Oxford University Press, 1986); R. F. Foster, *Modern Ireland 1600–1972* (London: Penguin, 1989); Ian McBride, *Eighteenth-Century Ireland* (Dublin: Gill and Macmillan, 2009); and Thomas Bartlett, *Ireland: A History* (Cambridge: Cambridge University Press, 2010).

Picture Credits

Every effort has been made to contact all copyright holders.
The publishers will be pleased to correct in future editions
any omissions brought to their attention.

1. Godfrey Kneller, portrait of George I in his coronation robes,
   1716 (Granger Collection/Alamy)
2. Map of the electorate of Hanover (Enacademic.com)
3. View of the gardens at Herrenhausen, *c.*1708 (Wikimedia Commons)
4. Elector Ernst August, Duke of Brunswick-Lüneburg, seventeenth
   century (Bomann-Museum, Celle/ Fine Art Images/Heritage Im-
   ages/Getty Images)
5. Electress Sophia of Hanover, late seventeenth century (S. K. H.
   Erbprinz Ernst August von Hannover, Herzog zu Braunschweig
   und Lüneburg, Schloss Marienburg)
6. Godfrey Kneller (attr.), portrait of George when Prince of Brunswick-Lüneburg, *c.*1680 (© Residenzmuseum im Celler Schloss/
   Bomann-Museum, Celle/Fotostudio Loeper)
7. Jacques Vaillant (attr.), portrait of Sophia Dorothea with her children Georg August, the future George II and Sophia Dorothea,
   the future Queen of Prussia, *c.*1690 (© Residenzmuseum im Celler Schloss/Bomann-Museum, Celle/Fotostudio Loeper)
8. English school, *A Royal Hunting Party at Göhrde*, 1725 (Royal
   Collection Trust © Her Majesty Queen Elizabeth II, 2016/Bridge-
   man Images)

Index